Take Away the Stone

Jesus Frees Us from Death

A Journey Through John 11

By Alan Sommer

PRESS

Take Away the Stone
Jesus Frees Us from Death
by Alan Sommer

Printed in the United States of America

ISBN 978-1-60477-755-0

www.xulonpress.com

To God be the glory!

I am filled with gratitude to Jesus Christ, my Savior, for giving me life now and forever. He has opened my heart and mind to the wonders of His grace and given me the sure and certain hope of the resurrection. If you, the reader, find any comfort in this book, it is because of Him. I pray that you also may be filled with the "inexpressible and glorious joy" of His gift of salvation.

I also thank Jesus for my incredible wife, who has supported me, prayed with me, and been a partner now these 15 years of marriage. She is a daily reminder of the Lord's love for me, and she is a far greater gift than I deserve. I am grateful to her and to our children for their patience as I worked on this project.

Thanks are also due to my parents for consistently teaching their children that every day begins and ends with the Lord. To them and all the family that God has grown through them, thank you.

Thank you to those who proof read, edited, and made wonderful suggestions too numerous for me to count.

Finally, I wish to thank God's people who have allowed me to witness their faith in Christ even when physical death approached. They helped me to see that the hope Jesus brings is real. May all glory be given to Him, for He is the way, the truth, and the life.

For Cheryl

Table Of Contents

Introduction

The Valley

One summer in the mid 1990s, my wife Beth and I loaded up the car and went on a vacation to the southwestern United States. We had an exciting itinerary all planned out. There were friends and relatives in southern California we wanted to visit. One of my wife's college roommates and her family lived in the Phoenix area, and I had a friend from seminary not too far away from them, so we had reason to go to Arizona as well. We had a great time seeing old friends and making new ones, staying up late to have the kind of conversations you wish you could have more often with people you love. We had time to visit museums and walk on the beach in southern California. We even were able to see the Grand Canyon! These were the BC years for Beth and me—Before Children!

But the time came when we had to head home. Because we had ended our visiting in Arizona, our way home led near a very famous valley. Death Valley.

Death Valley has an incredibly harsh climate, with high temperatures in the summer easily exceeding 100 degrees Fahrenheit. The animals that live there have adapted to living in extreme heat with very little water. On the National Park Service web page for Death Valley, it says, *"From 1931 through 1934, a 40 month period, only 0.64 inches of rain fell."* In the summer of 2001, there were 154 consecutive days when the high temperature was over 100° F! The summer of 1917 had 43 consecutive days at 120° F or above! Now that's hot!

It was a very interesting experience going through the desert. Any time we got out of the car to get gas, take a break, or eat, we were blasted by extreme heat! Even when we stopped at our motel around 9:00 or 10:00 pm that night, it was still around 100 degrees. For a boy raised in the Pacific Northwest, it felt very warm! After checking in we swam in the pool right away, then gratefully slept in an air conditioned room.

There is no way that I would try to cross this desert in the summer on foot. If I had to travel home without modern transportation, maps, and air conditioning, I believe the area would live up to its name: Death Valley. A valley of death.

Every one of us is on a journey called life. There is a lot to enjoy about living on this earth. We delight in seeing God's handiwork in creation, hiking in the mountains or smelling the salt water of the ocean. We savor the aroma and taste of a delicious meal, and listen with joy to music that stirs our souls. We treasure time spent with friends and family and long conversations into the night. We find deep joy and fulfillment in having a life's partner in marriage, in holding our first child, and growing more mature.

But some day this journey will take an inevitable turn toward a valley, called in Psalm 23:4 the *"valley of the shadow of death."* It is a valley that everyone has to enter, a place no one can avoid. There is no one who escapes this valley.

The Bible teaches us that there is a home prepared for us on the other side of this valley of the shadow of death. But to get there, we must make it through. Is there a way?

God is ready to take us on a journey, so that we might see things from His perspective. And as He does this, we will discover that He addresses some of the deepest longings of the human heart. Into the arid and harsh climate that death brings, God provides answers to some of the biggest questions mankind can ask.

So journey through the eleventh chapter of John with me. You might want to read John 11:1–53 all at once, or just a few verses at a time, as we work through each section of this book. Let God engage not only your mind but also your heart has you see His response to suffering and death. Travel with me to see a family in crisis, a family dealing first with a terminal illness, then the death of one of their own. See them suffer as a loved one gets sick and dies. Watch one family member, then another, pour out her grief and anguish to God.

You will see your own tears reflected in their weeping. You will hear them ask some hard questions. "God, why didn't you come in time to spare my brother's life?" "When I called out, why didn't you answer?" And these questions probably echo some of your own: "Lord, I'm not hearing you. Are you really there?" "Why did my wife have to die?" "What can I tell my sister after she lost her child?"

These are the questions of a suffering humanity. These are the anguished cries of the human heart when death makes a visit. But God wants to lead us through this dark valley to a place of hope and life.

Chapter 1

9-1-1

Something bad had happened. We weren't supposed to stop in the middle of the highway. I stepped hard on the brakes to avoid the other cars that had stopped in front of us. About a dozen vehicles were stopped right in the center of the freeway in the middle of the afternoon. There were dust clouds from cars driving on the median. My stomach tightened up as I anticipated what we might see.

That warm spring day my wife, Beth, and I were on the way to our local Home Depot. We had loaded our one-year-old daughter into our old Toyota Camry and had just pulled onto the highway near our home. We were thinking about home improvement projects and talking back and forth about what we wanted to do. However, God had a different project in mind for us that day.

We pulled off the highway onto the median with our flashers blinking and saw something horrific. There had been an accident. A large SUV had rolled over and was lying upside down in the road, metal crumpled. There was glass lying on the pavement, reflecting the light of the sun. And there was more.

A woman came running down a 50-foot embankment above the highway so she could help. I saw shocked and frightened expressions on the faces of the people in their cars. People were dialing on their cell phones, calling 9-1-1 for help. And then I saw why.

There were children lying on the pavement. Some were crying, some were lying still. The SUV had been carrying six children, plus the driver, when it careened out of control, hit the embankment, and rolled over. It was a scene I'll never forget.

There is something about an emergency like this that burns into our memories. We sense that the situation is critical. People are hurt. Lives are on the line. And we dial for help. We dial 9-1-1 when there is an automobile accident. We dial 9-1-1 when someone suffers a heart attack. We dial 9-1-1 when there is a crime committed or there is immediate danger. We dial 9-1-1 when we need help and protection.

9-1-1 is not one of my favorite number combinations. It's the number that most of us use only for emergencies. It's a number that we dial when there is an injury, an accident or a crime. When we dial 9-1-1, with adrenaline running and voices shaking, our worst fears may be materializing right in front of us.

I don't like to dial that number. But there are those times when 9-1-1 is the number we need to call.

9-1-1 is not just an emergency number, it's also a date, a day in history that will not be forgotten for a long, long time. 9-11-2001. September 11, 2001. A tragic day when 9-1-1 must have been dialed a thousand times. A day when thousands of people lifted up prayers to God, asking for help, asking hard questions. "Why did this happen?" "How do I go on?"

We struggle to answer those questions. As a pastor, I have learned some of what the Bible has to say. I have been taught different ways to deal with the question of evil in this world.

But when you experience it first hand, or when you see horrifying images on television, the words of "expert" commentators don't seem to be enough. As I saw the images of people falling hundreds of feet to their deaths, I couldn't say anything. As the twin towers fell in on themselves, killing thousands, I was in shock. To see death on such a massive scale, to see evil directly in action, is enough to close our mouths and silence our tongues. But deep inside, there is a burning question: Why? Why does it have to be this way? Why are there accidents? Why do we have to die?

Why Do We Have to Die?

The sad answer to that question is found in the first book of the Bible, Genesis. In chapters 1–2, we hear the wonderful story of creation. In six days, God created the heavens and the earth and everything that was in them. He rested from his work on the seventh day.[1] After each day of creation, the Bible tells us that God saw what He made, and it was good. After He finished His work of creation, we are told in Genesis 1:31 that *"God saw all that he had made, and it was very good."* The Bible often uses the number seven to describe something that is completed. So seven times the word "good" is used to describe God's perfect, complete creation.

A perfect humanity was part of that good creation. Our first parents, Adam and Eve, were sinless, just as God had created them. They were stewards of the earth, God's special creations, designed to be caretakers of the world God had placed them in.

But everything changed when they sinned. In Genesis 3, we read the tragic story of how Adam and Eve rebelled against God. He had placed them in a beautiful garden, the Garden of Eden, full of trees and delicious fruit. They could eat any of it—except for the fruit of one tree: the tree of the knowledge of good and evil. Here is what God told Adam:

> *"You are free to eat from any tree in the garden; but you must not eat from the tree of the knowledge of good and evil, for when you eat of it you will surely die."* [2]

This tree was a test of faith. It was God's way of reminding Adam that life came from God. Turning away from God would mean turning away from life.

Now, you would think with such plain language, Adam and Eve would have had no problems being loyal to the Lord. You might think that two perfect people living in one perfect garden on one perfect planet would be perfectly faithful. But this was not the case. Instead of relying on God's words, they listened to Satan.

"'You will not surely die,' the serpent said to the woman. For God knows that when you eat of it your eyes will be opened, and you will be like God, knowing good and evil.'" [3]

Instead of trusting their perfect Creator, they trusted their own judgment:

"When the woman saw that the fruit of the tree was good for food and pleasing to the eye, and also desirable for gaining wisdom, she took some and ate it. She also gave some to her husband, who was with her, and he ate it." [4]

The consequences of their actions were devastating:

- Faith in God was replaced by fear (they tried to hide from God when He came looking for them in Genesis 3:8)
- Care for each other was replaced by conflict (Adam tried to blame Eve for his failure in Genesis 3:12)
- Death entered the world. God said to Adam, "*For dust you are and to dust you will return.*" [5]

The New Testament book of Romans puts it this way: "*Sin entered the world through one man, and death through sin, and in this way death came to all men, because all sinned.*" [6] Adam and Eve had turned away from the God who is life, and they began to die spiritually and physically.

Even the creation itself was put under the curse of sin. Paul writes in Romans 8, "*For the creation was subjected to frustration, not by its own choice, but by the will of the one who subjected it, in hope that the creation itself will be liberated from its bondage to decay and brought into the glorious freedom of the children of God.*" [7]

Notice the words and concepts we see in these Bible readings: Fear. Frustration. Bondage. Decay. And the biggest word of all: Death. The Scripture is very clear on this subject. These are the horrible consequences of our sin. Along with Satan, we are to blame for the problems in our world. Our ultimate enemy, death, is the result of our sinful condition.

And so we witness fatal accidents. A loved one is diagnosed with a terminal illness. And eventually, we all end up at the same destination—death. Where can we turn for help in life's emergencies? Does God have an answer when death invades our lives?

We Are Not Alone

The incredible message of the Bible is that we are not alone as we face sin and death. Even as Adam and Eve hid from God in their sin and shame, He came looking for them. Genesis 3:8-9 tells us part of the story.

"Then the man and his wife heard the sound of the LORD God as he was walking in the garden in the cool of the day, and they hid from the LORD God among the trees of the garden. But the LORD God called to the man, 'Where are you?'"

Isn't that incredible? Adam and Eve had just completely blown it. Yet God didn't walk away, He walked toward them! Their sin had ushered death into God's perfect creation, but He didn't immediately destroy them! Instead, He came looking for them. He still had a purpose for their lives.

My friends, the story of the Bible is not about people looking for God. It is the story of God looking for His lost people. God sees the pain and suffering that death brings. He hears the cries of His hurting people.

When you are blinded by the pain of losing a loved one, God calls out, "Where are you?" When you receive that terrible phone call and your heart is broken, God says, "Where are you?" He is looking for you because He loves you. He will send a friend who will listen to your pain and pray with you. He will bring healing to the deepest recesses of your heart through a Bible passage that comes alive and speaks to you like never before. A Christian song or hymn will touch your soul in a way that brings healing and joy from

God, a joy that you thought you could never feel again. God hears your cry, and He responds.

It's amazing to see how God answers our cries for help. On that warm afternoon when my wife and I witnessed the automobile accident, He began helping immediately.

I ran to the first medical people on scene, identified myself as a pastor, and asked how I could help. I was asked to sit with the woman who had been driving the SUV.

She was sitting on a blanket and had seriously injured her foot. She was shaking. On that warm, comfortable day, she was trembling like it was winter in Minnesota and she didn't have a coat. I held her hand and my arm shook from the force of her trembling. But it wasn't just the pain in her foot that caused her to have tremors. Her pain was as emotional as it was physical. I quickly found out why.

Her three children had been passengers in that car, along with her sister's three kids. And she could hear them crying. My heart was filled with grief for her, as I thought of my own little girl, sitting safely in our car, not a hundred feet away.

We prayed. And we were not alone. God had sent another Christian pastor onto that same highway that same day. We each held one of her hands, and we prayed. We dialed 9-1-1 to God. We prayed for the safety of the children. We prayed for the medical workers on the scene. And we prayed for this dear woman, already racked with guilt and fear, panic stricken at what had happened. God was there, right in the midst of the emergency, bringing help.

God has something to show us here. It is when we are at our weakest that God shows His strength. It is when we have no answers that God's wisdom shines through. He cares about your suffering. The problems of sin and death are not problems that we face alone. When we call out for help to God, He hears us.

So let's take a walk through John 11 together, and see how God responds to the deepest needs of mankind. We won't understand everything. But I promise the journey will be worthwhile. For help is on the way. God has already heard our prayers, heard the prayers of all humanity. And He has sent an answer.

Chapter 2

Statistics Have Names

S ome years ago I knew a wonderful hospice worker by the name of Alma. I admired her a great deal, as she tirelessly worked with others, making every effort to help the dying person and his or her family. What was so wonderful was how she treated the people she worked with. To her, they were more than just clients or patients. They were people she grew to know and to love.

Alma is like a lot of the hospice workers I have met over the years. They have been wonderful caregivers. A hospice worker walks into a home where someone is terminally ill, someone who is a complete stranger. From a statistical perspective, the patient is a number, another victim of pancreatic cancer or congestive heart failure. But for people like Alma, that person has a name, a family and a life.

When your family is touched by death, you discover that death is an intensely personal experience. When a close friend receives a diagnosis that is terminal, it is not simply statistical information. The news brings a flood of emotions and a whole range of reactions.

Terminal illness and death affect real people every day. These real people are our neighbors, our co-workers, our fellow students. And they are our family members.

Statistics have names. This is one of the lessons we first learn from John 11. When we begin reading this chapter, we are reminded that death is personal.

"Now a man named Lazarus was sick. He was from Bethany, the village of Mary and her sister Martha." [8]

Oh, it starts off sounding a little impersonal. Literally translated, this verse begins, "There was someone who was sick." At first, we might think this story is just about showing how Jesus is going to do some miracle again. Maybe I would write it this way: "Some guy was ill." (I think it's a good thing I didn't write John 11—don't you?)

That sounds pretty distant, doesn't it? That sounds a lot like what we hear almost every day. The nightly news begins with 10 or 15 minutes of what I call "the police report". We hear about the accidents, the murders, the assaults, the rapes, the deaths in war, and the latest terrorist news.

For most of us, it is impersonal. We don't know the family that was killed in the accident. It wasn't our cousin who was murdered. And so day after day, death can seem to be distant and far-off. We hear a news report about some new cancer drug, and we don't give it a second thought. We read about a new treatment for heart disease, and we just skim the article.

But all that changes when someone we love becomes terminally ill or dies. Sickness and death are always remote forces, things that other people have to deal with, until they affect us.

When your mother calls you to say that Dad is having heart problems, you want to know everything. When your brother says that he has prostate cancer, you want to find out what the treatment options are. It's different when the sick one is in your family. It's different when the disease strikes home. Suddenly, it's personal.

And the ultimate "personal touch" of death occurs when we are the ones getting the diagnosis. After the doctor says, "You have pancreatic cancer, and you probably have two to six months to live," death isn't a remote force any longer. When you come to the shocking realization that Alzheimer's or HIV have begun their one way trips to the grave with your body in tow, it hits you right between the eyes.

Everything changes when we face our own mortality. Suddenly, we want to know more about how cancer works and what the chances for survival are. We start thinking of our loved ones and how this illness will affect them. And we start wondering about how we will die—and if there is any hope for life.

The Context of Death

Chapter 11 of John begins by saying, "There was someone who was sick." In fact, as we will soon discover, he was more than sick, he was terminally ill. As the story begins, the description of the man seems pretty impersonal. But as we look more closely at verse one, we discover a very personal context.

This man has a name, and his name is Lazarus. He is a real man from a real town called Bethany, a suburb of Jerusalem. This is a personal story for him. He has a family, two sisters he is very close to. He has a life. He has a home. And this illness is hitting where it hurts.

He and his sisters knew that life was ebbing away. Perhaps he wondered just how many more sunrises he would see. Maybe he worried about who would care for his sisters after he was gone. Did he feel lonely as he became more and more ill, finding himself more and more isolated from his friends? Did he feel useless, like a burden, as he became weaker and weaker, unable to feed himself, eventually unable even to get up and go to the bathroom?

How many times did Lazarus call out to God in prayer, asking for a reprieve, a second chance? How many doctors did he see, hoping that one of them would know of something that could help?

In John 11, Lazarus is not a statistic: he is a man, a brother, and a friend to others. He is a human being traveling through the most difficult place that any of us will go. He is walking through the valley of the shadow of death. He is facing the brutal reality that the Bible teaches us: *"Death has come to all people, because all have sinned."* [9] His journey would be a personal one.

Oh, yes, death is very personal. When you go on that last journey, it will, in all likelihood, be the greatest challenge you will ever face. It will be a severe test for your family and your closest friends. And you will want to be ready.

Every day of our lives, we make plans about how to use the time. Some of those plans revolve around our vocations as parents, workers, students. "Today is laundry," we think, "and tomorrow is grocery shopping." "I have to get that presentation completed by 3:00 tomorrow afternoon."

Some of our plans revolve around events. Next week is vacation. Next month is graduation. Next year I am getting married. Other plans focus on the needs of those we love the most. The kids will need new clothes for another school year. The kids will need new loans for another year at college!

And we have our long-term plans, plans for things we hope will happen a long way down the road. So we look over our investments to make sure we are ready for retirement. In every stage of life, we make plans—and that's good.

But when death comes close to home, suddenly things are different. You probably won't feel ready, because death is not a statistic any longer, it has become personal. Your friend, your brother or sister, your spouse, your parent or your child is dying. And ultimately you and I will have to take this journey, too.

But let me give you some hope. The very personal journey of death is one that God also takes very personally. You see, in verses two and three of John 11, we see the close connection between Lazarus and his family, and Jesus.

You Matter to Jesus

Jesus was a very important figure in the lives of Mary, Martha, and Lazarus. He had touched their family in significant ways, and it showed in the way they related to Him.

> *"This Mary, whose brother Lazarus now lay sick, was the same one who poured perfume on the Lord and wiped his feet with her hair. So the sisters sent word to Jesus, 'Lord, the one you love is sick.'"* [10]

Mary had shown her faith and devotion to the Lord by pouring expensive perfume on His feet and wiping His feet with her hair.

Now, with their brother in need, the sisters reached out to the One they knew would help. Mary and Martha sent a message to Jesus. *"Lord, the one you love is sick,"* they said.

Note how personal this message is: "Jesus, your friend is dying. We are calling out to you." This doesn't sound like an HMO request for medication: "Patient number 843–322–22444–111 is requesting authorization for medication 324B." This is a personal plea for help.

Yes, Jesus was important to Mary, Martha, and Lazarus, just as He is important to you. But even better, Lazarus, Mary and Martha were important to Jesus. He would come. He would respond. Their suffering and their sorrow mattered to Him. Lazarus's illness meant something to Jesus.

To Jesus, Lazarus wasn't a statistic; he was a friend in need. To Jesus, Lazarus wasn't a footnote in a news article; he was a child of God who was calling out to his Lord. And his Lord would respond.

Never, ever forget this: you matter to Jesus. Your life is something that He created, something He gave you. He knows the numbers of hairs on your head and the number of worries in your heart. When your mother is dying and hospice has been called, He knows. When you see the signs of age staring back at you from the mirror, Jesus sees them too. When you fear for your children's future because you know your time is short, your Savior knows the burden of anxiety you bear. And He cares. When you call out to Him, He hears.

There are so many marvelous stories in the Bible that illustrate this. Let me share just one with you, from Mark 10:46-52.

Then they came to Jericho. As Jesus and his disciples, together with a large crowd, were leaving the city, a blind man, Bartimaeus (that is, the Son of Timaeus), was sitting by the roadside begging. When he heard that it was Jesus of Nazareth, he began to shout, "Jesus, Son of David, have mercy on me!" Many rebuked him and told him to be quiet, but he shouted all the more, "Son of David, have mercy on me!" Jesus stopped and said, "Call him." So they called to the blind man, "Cheer up! On your feet! He's calling you."

Throwing his cloak aside, he jumped to his feet and came to Jesus. "What do you want me to do for you?" Jesus asked him. The blind man said, "Rabbi, I want to see." "Go," said Jesus, "your faith has healed you." Immediately he received his sight and followed Jesus along the road.

It sure seemed like poor old Bartimaeus didn't stand a chance. He was on the side of the road, begging for whatever he could get. To most people, he was one of the invisible members of society, a poor beggar to be ignored whenever possible. Jesus was surrounded by His disciples and a large crowd. People were talking to Jesus and asking Him questions. Perhaps some of the disciples were debating with several Pharisees. It was crowded and noisy, like a crowded city sidewalk in the middle of the day.

Bartimaeus couldn't see, so he didn't know quite where to aim his voice as he called out. Others told him to be quiet. It appeared as if nobody cared about Bartimaeus and what he had to say. Who could possibly hear him above the noise of the crowd?

Jesus could. In the midst of a large crowd of noisy people, Jesus heard one lone voice. When the world had judged that Bartimaeus was to be quiet, Jesus wanted him to speak up.

Maybe you are young and your health is great. You exercise five times a week, you eat right, and you have strength and energy to spare. But a day will come, and maybe your day isn't too far away, when you will realize that your time on this earth is short. A day will come when all of those plans you made just won't matter anymore. A day when doing laundry is irrelevant and your job won't be a concern. A day when investments in the things of this world will pale in comparison to investments made in eternal things. A day when your retirement won't be needed any longer.

And you will call out to God, and your family will call out with you, "Lord, the one you love is sick." You might wonder, "Does He really love me? Can God still love me, after all those times when I have turned a cold shoulder to Him? Can God still love me, after all the wrong I have done, after all the good I have failed to do?"

Alleluia! The answer of the Savior is an unqualified "Yes!" He does love you—with all of His heart. He does hear you, and He wants you to speak up. Jesus loves you, and because He loves you, He takes death and dying very seriously. And very personally. So personally that He has traveled that dark valley Himself. He has approached His last day, His last hour, and His last breath. Death is very personal for Jesus, for He has experienced it.

Why did He experience death? He did it for you. Romans 4:25 says, *"He was delivered over to death for our sins and was raised to life for our justification."*

You are not a statistic to Jesus. You are not a line item in a report. You are His beloved child. He went to a cross for you. He faced and defeated death for you, because He loves you. And He hears when you call. You have a name—and Jesus knows it.

Chapter 3

Is God on Vacation?

In the early years of my pastoral ministry, I received a phone call informing me that a young woman was dying. I was asked to come to the hospital, to go to the bedside of a dying child of God. This is something that by God's grace pastors and other believers have the opportunity to do. We are blessed and privileged to see the miracle of God's Word working comfort, hope, and life, even as people die.

I really enjoy what I do as a pastor. The times when I am able to encourage sorrowing people with the hope Jesus brings are so wonderful and fulfilling. But sometimes it is very difficult. This was one of those times.

The woman who was dying wasn't old. She hadn't lived a long and fruitful life. She wasn't ready to die, hadn't set her affairs in order. She was young. She was a 31-year-old mother on her second marriage. Her first marriage had been a struggle. She had experienced a lot of pain. The one joy that she had from her first marriage was her daughter, who was now about seven years old.

After her divorce, she had remarried happily. This marriage, praise God, had brought her joy. She had a closeness with her husband that she had never experienced before. She had a husband who supported and loved both her and her daughter.

But now, at age 31, she was dying of cancer. The cancer had moved so fast that there hadn't been much time for chemotherapy or other treatments. Her body was still strong. She didn't want to die. The God-given instinct to live was powerful, and her body wasn't about to give up without a fight.

So there we were in the hospital, hour after agonizing hour. This was not the death of a very elderly person at the end of a long and peaceful life. There would be no peaceful falling asleep and waking up in heaven. This was a battle between life and death. And we all knew the ultimate outcome.

The doctors did their best with medication to control the pain. Thankfully, the young woman was unconscious and unaware of what was going on. But still, her body struggled.

It started Friday afternoon. The family informed me that the doctors were saying it would be just a few hours. So I stayed. A couple of hours later, there was no end in sight. Family members took turns in the hospital room, so that others could get a break. I went home for a quick bite of dinner and came back. There was still no dramatic change, no sign that death would come swiftly.

Friday evening passed into Saturday morning. I had visited throughout the night. The family kept their constant vigil, giving each other food breaks, walking breaks, sanity breaks.

When I came into the hospital Saturday afternoon, more than 24 hours after the doctors had said this young woman would die, her mother approached me. She had anger in her eyes and anger in her heart. Her anger was directed at God, and I happened to be the one trying to show God's comfort to her. She had questions that went through me like a high powered rifle bullet would rip through paper. "Is God on vacation? Why won't He let my daughter die?"

You can understand her feelings! After the pain of her daughter's divorce, this grieving mother had rejoiced to see her child finally find happiness in married life. And cancer was taking it all away. What would become of her seven-year-old granddaughter? How would her daughter's husband deal with the loss? And to add insult to injury, her daughter's death was slow, painful, and agonizing.

Her questions raised questions in my own heart, questions I wondered if I would be able to answer. What could I say now that could help? And what would I say at the funeral?

Bullets of Anger

Maybe you have heard those kinds of questions before. Maybe you have asked them. Have you fired a bullet of anger at God, when you realized that your husband was going to die? Have you reached the end of your hope when the doctor told you that the leukemia was raging unchecked in your daughter's body?

These are not the detached questions of a philosophical discussion or a seminary classroom. These are the anguished outcries of the people of God, as they struggle with sin, dying, and death.

What about it? What about all those fervent prayers? What about the hundreds of Christian friends who have prayed on your behalf? What about the prayer chains and the email prayers sent to thousands of people who are praying? When nothing seems to improve, what can we say? What is going on? Why won't God answer me? Is He on vacation?

I wonder if that's how Mary and Martha felt.

So the sisters sent word to Jesus, "Lord, the one you love is sick." When he heard this, Jesus said, "This sickness will not end in death. No, it is for God's glory so that God's Son may be glorified through it." Jesus loved Martha and her sister and Lazarus. Yet when he heard that Lazarus was sick, he stayed where he was two more days. [11]

Out of their sorrow, their desperation, the two sisters sent out a call for help to Jesus. They were doing the right thing. They asked for help from the right person. Their friend Jesus was the miracle worker from Nazareth. He had healed countless others. And He had proven that He could handle even death. He had raised a little girl from the dead, and brought back to life the son of a grieving widow.[12] He claimed to be the very Son of God. Jesus was the One to ask for help. Jesus could bring the life-saving power of God to help their sick brother.

Yes, sending for Jesus was the thing to do. Not only did He have the power to help them, He was their friend. Indeed, verse five tells us that *"Jesus loved Martha and her sister and Lazarus."* Yet initially, Jesus did nothing. He stayed where He was for two more days.

Let me ask you something. If your brother were dying and you called 9-1-1, how would you feel if there was no response for two days? If you went to the Emergency Room at your local hospital with a dying child, how would you react if no one did anything for a couple of days?

You wouldn't put up with it! There would be press coverage and maybe even lawsuits. You would be angry, and rightly so! People who deal with emergencies cannot take vacations when lives are at stake. But Jesus stayed right where He was when He received the call for help—for two days. Why? Was He on vacation?

You Call This Love?

Jesus stayed where He was because He loved them. Let me say that again: Jesus stayed right where He was *because He loved them.*

This doesn't seem to make any sense. Yet this is exactly what the text says. Jesus loved them, but *"when He heard that Lazarus was sick, He stayed where He was two more days."* How can we come to grips with this? The actions of Jesus don't seem to agree with the statement that He loved them.

The problem is that we see love with our very human eyes. We define love on our terms, with what makes sense to us. Jesus had a different kind of love for this family. The word translated here as "love" comes from the Greek New Testament word *agape*, a word that denotes the unconditional and sacrificial love of God. It is this love that prompted Him to send His Son for us. Because He loved Mary, Martha, and Lazarus with this kind of deeper, Godly love, He did not give them what they wanted—He gave them what they really needed. He did not give them a simple, temporary healing. Instead, as we will see later, His love for them led Him to give them something much grander and much bigger.

Jesus loved Martha, Mary, and Lazarus so much that He wanted them to see the bigger picture. Their idea of love looked for an immediate reprieve from suffering and death. The love of Jesus motivated Him to give them a permanent solution. So while God does not enjoy suffering and does not prolong our agony just for kicks, He does work through our pain when it will make us stronger and serve His purposes.

My friend Mike was a mechanic, a guy who loved cars. He worked on them and he raced them. He was a hard worker who had a rough exterior, with language to match.

Then Jesus took hold of Mike. God showed Mike that He loved him, in a way that Mike could understand. He started worshipping regularly and reading his Bible. Jesus became a personal friend to Mike, and it changed his life. The rough edges became a little softer, although Mike, like all of us, was always a work in progress.

When Mike was diagnosed with pancreatic cancer, it was very hard on him and his family. The entire racing community heard the bad news. But they also heard good news. Mike just had to tell anyone who would listen about his Savior. He knew he had eternal life, and he wanted others to experience the joy and peace he had as he faced his own mortality. God worked through Mike's witness to bring people to faith and eternal life in Jesus. What looked like loss was used by God for victory.

This is one of the amazing things about our Savior. He sees the deeper struggle, the reality that our sinful condition is behind the suffering. He sometimes allows pain so that He can work the greater good. He uses what seems to be total loss for a bigger victory. He takes our human logic and turns it upside down.

The illness we read about in John 11 wasn't just about Lazarus and the fact that he would die. No, this was about God. This was about who Jesus is and what He does to death.

What we discover here is that the central character in this story isn't Lazarus or Martha or Mary. The central character is Jesus. As much as Jesus didn't want His three friends to suffer, He loved them enough to want to open their eyes, and ours, to who He was and is. So He waited where He was for two days. Because He loved them.

Jesus' words in verse four also help us come to grips with His actions. He said, *"This sickness will not end in death. No, it is for God's glory so that God's Son may be glorified through it."*

Jesus would use Lazarus as a powerful visual aid that would point to His identity. Oh, yes, Jesus loved this family. We will see later that He even wept at the tomb of His friend. He grieves over the power that death has in our lives. But He loved this family enough to show them that He is the main point. And He loves us enough that He wants us to see this same truth. The main story is not about Lazarus dying or about our deaths, says Jesus. *"It is for God's glory."*

In fact, this story really isn't even about death. It's about life. It's about the life that Jesus came to give and comes to give. It's about the amazing reality that Jesus holds our very lives in His hands, and He can raise us from the dead.

Does Jesus love us? You bet He does. He loves us so much that He wants us to see that God is the central character of our lives. We are not the stars of the show—Jesus is. And Jesus does not go on vacation, even though it might seem that way to us.

Not a God on Holiday

To help us understand that Jesus does not go on holiday, let's take a look at another chapter of John. In John 17:1, Jesus has an intimate dialogue with His Heavenly Father. He converses with His heavenly Father on a night filled with emotion—the night He was betrayed and arrested.

> *"After Jesus said this, he looked toward heaven and prayed: 'Father, the time has come. Glorify your Son, that your Son may glorify you.'"*

On the very night that Jesus would be betrayed into the hands of His enemies, Jesus talked again of being glorified, just as He did in John 11:4. But He would not be glorified in the way we think. To our way of thinking, being glorified means having people praise us, getting our names in the newspaper. Here again, Jesus turns things upside down. For Jesus, His time of being glorified meant something completely different. His time had come, the time for Him to give His life for the sins of the world.

His sweat was mingled with His own blood as He agonized over what the Father had asked Him to do. He prayed in the Garden of Gethsemane,

"My Father, if it is possible, let this cup pass from Me; yet not as I will, but as You will." [13]

The answer that He heard from His Father was clear. There was no other way. He had to die for us to live.

This was no vacation, no walk in the park for Jesus. This was not a God on holiday, but a Savior who was giving everything He had for the life of His people. Jesus, a young man in His early thirties, would lay down His life for Lazarus, Martha, and Mary. He would lay down His life for you and me.

And He would lay down His life for the thirty-one-year-old mother and her family with whom we began this chapter. He did this so that she could have eternal life and so that her family could have hope and peace. Jesus finds His glory in giving Himself for us, in going to a cross, in dying for the sins of the world.

That is what I shared with this young woman's family at her memorial service. I reminded them of what Jesus had done for them. I reminded them that God does not run from suffering, that their Savior personally knows the agonies of death.

Consider the contrasts between this thirty-one-year-old woman and the Savior who died in His early thirties:

- She died in a hospital. Jesus died on a cross.
- She had caring medical professionals doing their best to ease her pain. Jesus had professional soldiers doing their best to give Him pain.
- This young woman constantly had her family telling her they loved her. Jesus died with His enemies' taunts ringing in His ears.
- Her family held her in their gentle embrace. Jesus was held by nails to hard, unyielding wood, unable to be held by His mother.

- She was never left alone in her hospital room. Jesus had His Heavenly Father turn His back. He cried out, *"My God, my God, why have you forsaken me?"*

As the old hymn says, "Jesus knows our every weakness." He knows all our weaknesses because He carried them. God has not taken a holiday from our times of suffering. He has experienced our suffering, our sorrow, even our death. And because of that, we can take our every need to Him in prayer. This is beautifully expressed in Hebrews 4:15-16:

For we do not have a high priest who is unable to sympathize with our weaknesses, but we have one who has been tempted in every way, just as we are—yet was without sin. Let us then approach the throne of grace with confidence, so that we may receive mercy and find grace to help us in our time of need.

Jesus never took a day off because He desired to finish the work of our salvation. His hard work has given us an eternal holiday from death, a day when death will be forever swallowed up in victory. Until that day comes, we are reminded every time we worship that Jesus has given us the victory. There we hear again and again the story of God's creation, our fall into sin and death, and Jesus' saving work for us. Jesus, the living Messiah, is our life.

Jesus stayed away from Lazarus for a couple of days, so He could point to this enormous truth. In the death of Lazarus, God's Son would be glorified. In this death, Jesus could show His life.

Do you realize what this means for us? God's Son will be glorified in your death and mine, in the death of any Christian, because it is not the end. Yes, you and I will physically die some day. But God will be glorified in our resurrection, even as He was glorified when Lazarus was raised from the dead.

You are not alone—even when it feels like you are. Your Savior never takes a vacation from loving you.

Chapter 4

In Harm's Way

"I intend to go in harm's way." John Paul Jones

John Paul Jones is considered by many to be the father of the American Navy. He was born in Scotland, but served in the navies of the United States and Russia. During the American Revolutionary War, while serving in the United States Navy, he had an idea that seemed foolish to a lot of his contemporaries. He thought that one of the best ways to fight for independence was to carry the war to British waters. He intended to go and raid the British coastline, forcing them to keep forces, equipment, and supplies away from the American Colonies.

Others thought it was crazy to go into the heart of enemy territory. It seems that most strategists felt that every American ship should stay at home, to defend the colonists attempting independence.

You can understand their reluctance. According to the Naval Historical Center website,

The United States Navy traces its origins to the Continental Navy, which the Continental Congress established on 13 October 1775 by authorizing the procurement, fitting out, manning, and dispatch of two armed vessels to cruise in search of munitions ships supplying the British Army in America.

Two armed vessels is a pretty humble beginning for a navy. Most people would have played it safe, but John Paul Jones was not most people. He had a bold idea, and it was a successful one. His activities kept the British from keeping an effective blockade of the American East coast. His successes encouraged France to enter the war on the side of the colonies. And John Paul Jones captured the British ship *Drake*, the first enemy warship ever to surrender to a United States vessel.

John Paul Jones is famous for a line in a letter he wrote in November 1778: "I wish to have no connection with any ship that does not sail fast; for I intend to go in harm's way."

"I intend to go in harm's way." Not many of us would say that easily. Not many of us wish to seek out harm. It takes great courage and bravery to risk life and limb in serving one's country. I am very grateful to the many men and women of our country who have shown such courage that we might have the freedoms we do in the United States.

Travel Plans

But what if a person had to go alone into battle? What person could face an entire army? That would be crazy, suicidal even! That is exactly what Jesus' disciples thought when He suggested a return to Judea.

> *"Then he said to his disciples, 'Let us go back to Judea.'*
> *'But Rabbi,' they said, 'a short while ago the Jews tried to*
> *stone you, and yet you are going back there?'"* [14]

This was not a casual conversation between Jesus and His disciples. These were not the kind of carefree travel plans that you and I usually make.

This past summer my wife and I were trying to make vacation decisions. "Let's go to Seattle this summer." "Well, that won't work because of that wedding in Southern California the week before."

Casual conversation is for casual destinations. You probably talk in similar ways. "Let's go visit your folks this summer." "Let's go to Washington D.C.; I've always wanted to go." So you make your plans, you estimate the costs, you see if it will fit your budget. And you go if you are able.

But when Jesus says, "Let's go to Judea," He is making a dangerous statement. This is no casual conversation. The response of the disciples makes that very clear. "But Rabbi, they just tried to stone you. Why go back now?"

Indeed, when you look back in the Gospel of John, you discover that in chapter eight (8:59) and chapter ten (10:31), there were several attempts on Jesus' life. Many of the Jewish religious leaders were out to get Him. They weren't out simply to discredit Him or to embarrass Him publicly. They wanted Him dead. Judea was the last place He should return to. And yet here He was, going into the heart of enemy territory. Jesus intended to go in harm's way. Why? Jesus had a friend who needed waking up.

"After he had said this, he went on to tell them, 'Our friend Lazarus has fallen asleep; but I am going there to wake him up.' His disciples replied, 'Lord, if he sleeps, he will get better.' Jesus had been speaking of his death, but his disciples thought he meant natural sleep." [15]

The Ultimate Wake-Up Call

It isn't always easy to wake people up! Beth and I have two children, Abigail and David. At times it can be a struggle to encourage young ones that it really is in their best interest to go to sleep. But for our children at least, once they are out, they are out!

One night last year clearly illustrated what I am talking about. It was a warm fall evening, about ten o'clock at night. The kids had been asleep for a couple of hours, and Beth and I were thinking of our own pillows with longing. The windows were open, letting in the cool night air.

Unfortunately, that's not all they were letting in. There had been some grass fires burning upwind of us. They were not a threat to our city, but the smoke was something you could definitely see and smell.

Just after we had shut off the lights and had begun to rest, the smoke detector in our hallway went off. Let me tell you, the noise of that alarm caused adrenaline to shoot through every part of my body! I jumped out of bed, threw on the hallway light, grabbed a stool, and yanked out that battery as fast as I could. After Beth and I walked the house just to be sure there was no fire in our home, we finally tried to relax and to go back to sleep.

Oh, by the way, our children never did wake up. Not the incredible noise of the smoke detector, not the light in the hallway and not my running around woke those kids up! They slept through it all! Amazing! Sometimes you just can't wake people up.

Maybe you have raised kids and struggled to get them out of bed, especially in the teen years. Maybe you have to set three alarms to get yourself going in the morning. But can you imagine the challenge of waking someone from the sleep of death?

It would seem to be a waste of time. When people are dead, they're dead! You can use every alarm clock in the world, but a dead person is not going to wake up.

Jesus told His disciples that He had to wake up Lazarus. Because they didn't understand what He meant at first, Jesus had to explain that Lazarus was dead. He was going to wake him up from the sleep of death.

Think about that for a moment. That's a pretty profound statement, isn't it? What Jesus is saying here is that for Him, it is no more difficult waking someone from death than waking someone up from a nap. The voice of the Son of God is the alarm clock that even the dead hear and obey.

So Jesus would go into harm's way, into Judea, because His friends needed Him. He went because He had to wake up Lazarus from the sleep of death. He went because the death of Lazarus was a place to reveal God's glory and confirm the identity of Jesus, the Life-Giver.

He went to give life to Lazarus, but it would cost Jesus dearly. Lazarus would live, but Jesus would have to die. We have only to look near the end of John 11 to see the repercussions of Jesus' actions.

After Jesus had raised Lazarus to life, His enemies among the Jewish leadership met to discuss what to do. Here is what John reports of their conversation:

> *If we let him go on like this, everyone will believe in him, and then the Romans will come and take away both our place and our nation. Then one of them, named Caiaphas, who was high priest that year, spoke up, "You know nothing at all! You do not realize that it is better for you that one man die for the people than that the whole nation perish."* [16]

Jesus was going in harm's way. The raising of Lazarus was the last straw for Jesus' enemies, and they would find a way to kill Him. Jesus knew this, yet He went anyway.

What a comfort this is to us when a loved one is dying or when we are dying! There is nothing that can keep Jesus from our side. If He was not afraid to face a brutal crucifixion, He is not afraid to face our pain. If He did not shrink back from the anger of His enemies, He can handle the anger we feel over death. If He was willing to take on suffering and death so that we could wake up and live, He can handle our suffering and our dying.

There is no circumstance in life, there is no place we can go, there is no death we can die that will separate us from our Lord. This was the joy of the Apostle Paul, who wrote,

> *"For I am convinced that neither death nor life, neither angels nor demons, neither the present nor the future, nor any powers, neither height nor depth, nor anything else in all creation, will be able to separate us from the love of God that is in Christ Jesus our Lord."*[17]

This trust is the foundation of Christian living. Having a Savior like this is what gave Paul the courage to go on mission trips, to evangelize the lost, and to suffer all kinds of hardship. Listen to how Paul describes some of his sufferings:

Five times I received from the Jews the forty lashes minus one. Three times I was beaten with rods, once I was stoned, three times I was shipwrecked, I spent a night and a day in the open sea, I have been constantly on the move. I have been in danger from rivers, in danger from bandits, in danger from my own countrymen, in danger from Gentiles; in danger in the city, in danger in the country, in danger at sea; and in danger from false brothers. I have labored and toiled and have often gone without sleep; I have known hunger and thirst and have often gone without food; I have been cold and naked. Besides everything else, I face daily the pressure of my concern for all the churches.[18]

Where could Paul possibly find the strength to go on? How could he handle the danger, the exhaustion, the close brushes with death? He found that strength in Jesus. The Savior who went in harm's way to Judea, to raise Lazarus from the dead, was the same Savior who went with the Apostle Paul.

This is the Jesus who stands by your side. When the time comes for you to face the death of a family member or friend, Jesus stands with you. When you come to the realization that your life on this earth is not going to last much longer, the one who holds the keys of Death and Hades is at your side.[19] He went into harm's way, all the way to the cross and the grave for you. You are not alone in the danger you face.

And a day will come when Jesus will give you the grand wake-up call, the final alarm, on the day of the resurrection of all flesh. You will hear His voice and you will wake to eternal life!

Chapter 5

The News Nobody Wants

High schools in our area run a program called "Every Fifteen Minutes." It challenges teens and parents to recognize the dangers of driving under the influence of alcohol. An entire accident scene is set up in front of the school so that throughout the day students see what might happen. A couple of smashed up cars are brought to the high school. Students are asked to portray victims of a fictitious automobile accident. Some of them have broken arms or legs and wear splints and first aid workers attend to them as other students arrive at school. And some of the students in this "mini-drama" are fatalities. All day, every fifteen minutes, a student is removed from the classroom by someone dressed as the Grim Reaper. The idea is to show students the serious risks they are taking by drinking and driving.

Each year, teams of two–a law enforcement officer and a pastor–go out to visit parents as part of this program. They pair up to act as the messengers of bad news to the parents—a son or daughter has been killed in an automobile accident.

One year I was asked to participate in this program, and along with a member of the sheriff's department, we brought the (fictitious) news to these parents that their child had been killed. Even though these moms and dads knew it wasn't real, their reactions as parents were genuine. The emotions they expressed were not put on and the tears they cried were real. For these moms and dads, even the thought of their children dying was a fearful thing.

This is the news nobody wants to hear. "Your daughter was killed in an accident." "I'm sorry, your wife is dead. There was nothing we could do."

How do you respond when you get that news? When the phone rang in the middle of the night and you found out that your mother had died, how did you feel? When you raced to the hospital only to find out that you were too late, what emotions came to mind?

When the news of death comes, some people cry. Others go numb. I have seen outbursts of anger as well as uncontrollable sobbing and grief. Everyone reacts in his or her own way.

But in every situation, this is not a time for gladness. This is not a time when people celebrate. They cry real tears.

Yes, there can be a real sense of relief when a person dies, particularly after a long, painful illness at the end of a long, fruitful life. Yet, even here, the pain of separation is real. Death is no time for gladness. Or is it? Listen to what Jesus told His disciples: *"Lazarus is dead, and for your sake I am glad I was not there."* [20]

Jesus sure seems to get things backward. He says that He is glad He wasn't there! How can Jesus be glad at a time like this? Jesus loved Lazarus and his sisters! How can Jesus say He is glad when life has ebbed away from His friend Lazarus? This doesn't seem to be the caring Savior who is concerned for His people!

Do you ever question God's love for you? When you prayed and prayed and prayed that God would heal your aunt from cancer, but she died anyway, what do you do with that? Is this the loving God you have been told about? Is this the Jesus you have trusted in?

Unfortunately, times of suffering and sorrow can tempt us to question God's love for us. Perhaps we wonder if God is punishing us for a sin from the past. Maybe God is getting revenge now by taking someone from us. We wonder if He finally reached the end of His patience.

These are the questions that rob us of sleep and take away our sense of security. These are the doubts that would lead us away from faith in God to the bottomless pit of our anxieties. Do we have a God who loves us, or are we on our own when it comes to death? Do we have a God we can count on when death robs us of someone we love, or do we have to go it alone, because Jesus is glad He doesn't have to be there? Is there anything we can do to deal with death, or will we all lose at the finish?

Comeback

Probably the greatest rivalry in professional sports today is the baseball rivalry between the New York Yankees and the Boston Red Sox. You may not be a baseball fan, but their ongoing competition over the decades is fascinating.

On the one hand, the Yankees are arguably the most successful professional sports franchise ever. They have participated in more World Series championships, by far, than any other team. In fact, as of the date of this writing, the Yankees have appeared in 39 of the 101 World Series, winning 26! That is astounding! New York has also boasted the biggest names in baseball history, with players like Babe Ruth, Lou Gehrig, and Joe DiMaggio gracing their rosters.

On the other hand, the Boston Red Sox set a record for futility. They won the World Series way back in 1918, and then went on a prolonged drought. They actually traded away Babe Ruth to New York in 1918, and things went downhill after that. In 1986 they came so close to winning the World Series, but fell just short when a baseball went under first baseman Bill Buckner's glove.

And in so many recent years, it was the Yankees who kept them from winning. In the 1990s and early 2000s, it was the Yankees who eliminated them from the playoffs so many times.

In the 2004 playoffs, it seemed as if it couldn't get any worse. After a very successful regular season, the Red Sox were on the verge of being eliminated by the Yankees. Again. In a best of seven series, they were down three games to zero. They were down to the last inning, facing Mariano Rivera, the pitcher who is probably the all time best at closing out a game. Red Sox fans could feel another season slipping away. Yet another season would end in futility and frustration.

Inexplicably, the unthinkable, the impossible happened. Boston tied the game, and then won in extra innings. They won the next game. And the next. Unbelievably, Boston came back and won four straight games, ushering them into the World Series, where they won four straight again and claimed the title of world champions.

What happened? One of their players said it very well. He said that they always believed they could win. Their confidence in each other never wavered, even when it seemed impossible. Coming back from what appeared to be certain defeat to their nemesis gave the Red Sox supreme confidence—and they won the World Series easily.

There is no greater defeat than death for us human beings. Death is not just the bottom of the ninth inning for us. It's the ultimate loss, one that every person experiences. When we lose that battle, it appears that this is the end for us.

So when the disciples heard that Lazarus was dead, that was it: game over, career over, life over. But Jesus knew there was more. And that is why He was glad. He said, *"For your sake I am glad I was not there, so that you may believe."*

Jesus was about to pull off an amazing comeback. He was about to snatch life out of the jaws of death. His disciples (and many others) would be amazed. But more than that, they would hear a clear call to believe that Jesus was the Messiah, the messenger of life from God, sent to a world wrapped up in death.

He was glad that He was not there to heal Lazarus, for the sake of the disciples, so that He could show them who He really was:

- By raising Lazarus, Jesus turned permanent defeat into victorious life.
- By raising Lazarus, Jesus showed where life really comes from.

Jesus was not glad *because* Lazarus died; He was glad that He could work *through* his death. This is the astonishing truth Jesus shows us here: Jesus can work through our deaths!

Jesus is not glad when someone you care about dies. He does not rejoice when you die either. But He is glad when He can show us that He brings life out of death.

And He is glad to give you that life. That's why Jesus was walking that dusty road to Bethany. He was on His way to Jerusalem to give His life for our sin and our death. Remember, that was no easy task. The prayers and sweat and blood were real. But despite the agony, Jesus would go to a cross for you and me. It made Him glad; it gave Him joy to think of how He might save us.

> *"Let us fix our eyes on Jesus, the author and perfecter of our faith, who for the joy set before him endured the cross, scorning its shame, and sat down at the right hand of the throne of God."* [21]

So here it is: When the news seems to be at its worst, Jesus is at His best. When the phone call gives a message of death, God's living Word, Jesus, continues to give His life.

Jesus isn't afraid to go to Lazarus's grave. *"But let us go to him,"* He says. And Jesus isn't afraid to go to our graves.

For Jesus would go to His own grave. Jesus would be laid in a borrowed tomb. But He would rise from death and win the greatest comeback victory of all time. And He calls us to be a part of His team. It just seems a little backward.

> *"Then he said to them all: 'If anyone would come after me, he must deny himself and take up his cross daily and follow me.'"* [22]

The road to life leads through the death of Jesus Christ. Jesus calls on His followers also to die to sin, that He might give them life. Even as Lazarus died before the Lord gave him new life, we too must die before Jesus makes us alive.

> *"We were therefore buried with him through baptism into death in order that, just as Christ was raised from the dead through the glory of the Father, we too may live a new life."* [23]

The life of the Christian is viewed through the lens of the death and resurrection of Jesus. We live as people who are dead to sin, who have already died with Christ. We know by faith that we will be raised from the dead by our living, resurrected Savior. So we have confidence, even when things look bad. We have hope, when others might be in despair. Like a baseball team full of confidence even when things look bad, believers in Jesus can look death square in the eye and claim victory. Jesus has won the championship, and He shares His victory with us.

That's why some of the most powerful witnessing is done by Christians near their times of death. When a Christian can look a friend in the eye and say, "I'm not afraid because Jesus has given me eternal life," that is powerful. When a follower of the Savior can face his or her own pain, sorrow, and death with courage and faith, people notice.

Jesus will work through your death. He will face the bad news with you. And you won't be alone when you die. When it's the bottom of the ninth and death has you down to your last breath, when it appears to the world that you have lost, Jesus will deliver you into the eternal victory celebration. It's that simple. Death loses. Jesus wins. And you play on His team.

Chapter 6

Just Show Up

Iserved my pastoral internship out in the cornfields of Michigan, in the midst of a marvelous congregation and community. Being a city boy from Seattle, I was definitely in a different world as I drove into Michigan. Looking out the window I saw corn plants and a Lutheran church. A few miles down the road I saw a Lutheran church and some corn plants. Later on, there was more corn. And more Lutheran churches. I was not on the West coast any more! And I was not in a big city any more when I entered the town of Clio, Michigan. One stoplight. Around 2,000 people. Things were going to be different!

I had a fantastic year, however, learning so much from God's people at Messiah Lutheran Church. There is something about rubbing elbows with God's people that is good for any pastoral student. It's good for all of us, as together we work and succeed and fail and always come back to God's grace.

That was a lesson I learned almost immediately. I had been there only two weeks when one of our members lost her adult son in an automobile accident. In terms of pastoral experience, I was as green as the Michigan cornfields in the spring. I was not just scared, I was terrified. You see, our pastor had been out of town and was returning on the day of the accident. He was able to meet with the grieving mother on that terrible Friday, but he was leaving town again Sunday afternoon, right after church. There would be a viewing of the body Sunday night and the funeral a day or two later.

While I had another pastor to help me with the funeral, I would be on my own for the viewing on Sunday night. This would be the first time that this woman was going to see the body of her son. And the accident had been very violent. The funeral home staff had done a good job, but some reconstruction had been necessary.

What could I possibly say or do? What words of wisdom or comfort could I offer? I felt hopelessly out of my league and was terror stricken at the thought of failing this dear sister in Christ.

Fortunately for me, I had a wise supervising pastor. He reminded me that Jesus was in charge, and I was there simply to show the love of Jesus to the family and friends. He said something to the effect, "Prepare a short Bible verse of comfort and peace. Be ready to pray. But more than anything, just be there. It's okay for people to cry or scream or sob. Sometimes the best thing to do is simply to be there, to be present."

He was right. I learned an important lesson that day. Sometimes being there is as important as anything else you can do. After all, that's one of the ways Jesus cares for us. He uses us to show His love to each other.

"Bethany was less than two miles from Jerusalem, and many Jews had come to Martha and Mary to comfort them in the loss of their brother." [24]

The Comfort of Presence

In verse 19 of John 11, we read about people who came to Martha and Mary to comfort and encourage them. We don't know what they said or did, but you can be sure that they were a big help to the two sisters as they attempted to cope with their grief. Some of the people probably brought food. Others may have shared special memories they had of Lazarus. Perhaps someone offered a special thought that he had written down. The thing is, the friends of this family showed up.

Does anybody really want to go to a funeral? Probably not. It is sad that we lose people we love. We would much rather be working or doing something fun around the house, instead of dealing with death. But when we attend a memorial service, our presence says something loud and clear: we care.

We need to go! What a difference it makes when a brother or sister in Christ comes to grieve with us. When a friend from church brings a big salad and a big hug, she is showing her love. When an elder or deacon comes early to help out with the service, he is saying, "I love you in Christ." When the body of Christ gathers together in worship to hear the words of life from the living Savior and to sing the songs of resurrection, this is God's love in action. Jesus sends these people to be present, that He might show His love to us in very tangible ways. Everyone needs this kind of love from others when loss hits hard.

Someone showed me that love during a time of great loss. My wife and I were in the long and slow process of adopting our second child, Nathan. He had been placed in our home through an agency working in the county. The social worker was happy. We were happy. Nathan had bonded with us and with our daughter, Abigail. Everything was going smoothly, as we had hoped and prayed that it would.

Two months into our foster son's time with us everything unraveled. Another family had gone to court to force the child to be placed with them. This is every adoptive family's worst nightmare, and as foster/adoptive parents, we had little or no legal rights. We couldn't even be present in the courtroom as Nathan's fate was decided. After about three weeks, the decision was made. Nathan would be leaving us. Two days later he was gone.

It was like a death in the family. Our two-and-a-half-year-old daughter didn't sleep through the night for two weeks. My wife cried daily, and I was filled with a helpless rage. I had been unable to protect my family, unable to prevent this from happening.

Two months later our emotional wounds were still very fresh, yet life went on. I was attending a conference where the room was very crowded. All the seats were taken, so I sat on the floor in the back of the motel conference room. A fellow pastor, a friend of mine, saw me there and walked over to see me. He knew what our family had recently gone through. As he came over to me, I reached out to shake his hand. Without saying a word, he brushed my hand away, kneeled on the floor, and gave me a great big bear hug as the tears came to my eyes.

Without using words, my friend showed his love and his care for me. He came over to me, not caring that he was in the middle of a conference room, not caring that he had to get down on the floor to comfort me, not caring what other people might think. He came to me when I was hurting.

God With Skin On

When you lose someone to death, Jesus comes to you. That is the point of the Incarnation, the "En–flesh–ment" of God's Son. God put on flesh and became man in Jesus Christ so that we would not be alone in our losses. The Son of God came to a world filled with death, grieving over death. God put skin on so that by offering His body as a sacrifice, sin could be paid for. God put skin on, so that by physically rising from the dead, death itself could die.

God still shows up with skin when we need Him most, when we face death. First Corinthians 6:19 says, *"Do you not know that your body is a temple of the Holy Spirit, who is in you, whom you have received from God?"* When God sends other people, He comes along. Their love is God's love in action.

We have a ministry at our congregation called Stephen Ministry. Lay people are trained in Christian care giving, so that they might show the love of Jesus to those who are hurting. I just love one of the phrases that is used in Stephen Ministry training: "Stephen Ministers show up."

That's what God did for us. God showed up when Jesus put on flesh. God showed up when Jesus was baptized and began His ministry. God showed up for the sick, the guilty, and the possessed, as He gave healing and forgiveness. In the Messiah, God showed up to give life instead of death.

And God shows up in other people. Mary and Martha's friends showed up to comfort them. And you and I are called by the Lord Himself to show up when a brother or sister in the Lord dies, when a brother or sister in the Lord is grieving over a death that personally affects them.

Maybe you don't feel like you know what to say. Maybe you aren't sure what to do. Maybe you feel as green as a Michigan cornfield in the spring. Just go. Show up. Share the Word of God. And remember that you don't go alone. Jesus will show up with you.

Chapter 7

Where Is the Resurrection?

I want to tell you about Chuck and Luana. Chuck and Luana were a marvelous Christian couple who loved to serve the Lord. They were dedicated Sunday School teachers, who loved those third and fourth grade students. Each week they would faithfully prepare their lesson, praying that God would guide them and the children. Each week they also faithfully worshipped with the body of Christ at their congregation. They were loved and respected by many in the church.

Over the years, Chuck's work had led them to live in a number of cities. Now, in their retirement, they were able to travel to see relatives and friends. They loved to visit former congregations and re-connect with loved ones.

It was on one of these trips that Chuck suffered a massive heart attack and died. It was very unexpected, for he and Luana made sure to exercise every day and eat right. Yet it happened anyway.

As I visited in the weeks following Chuck's death, Luana said something that struck me as powerfully instructive for the rest of us. She said that although she was grieving and in great pain, she knew she was going to be okay. All the years of devotional time, worship, and Bible reading were bearing fruit. She knew where to turn when tragedy struck. She knew Jesus was there for her when she needed Him.

She reminds me a lot of Martha in John 11. Martha had also experienced tragedy. She was in the midst of the kind of grief that only a death in the family can bring. How would she cope? Where would she turn? We see in verses 21–22 that she would turn to Jesus.

"Martha then said to Jesus, 'Lord, if You had been here, my brother would not have died. Even now I know that whatever You ask of God, God will give You.'" [25]

The time that Jesus had spent with Martha and her family was bearing fruit. His teaching and preaching, the hope that poured out from His words, the manner in which He loved others—all of this had created a living and powerful faith in Martha. Now, at this most painful moment in her life, her faith pointed to the One who could help her. And she expressed that faith with profound words: "Even now I know that whatever You ask of God, God will give You."

Martha put the very life of her brother into the hands of Jesus. She recognized that Jesus could have turned around a terminal illness. She acknowledged that when Jesus prays, when the Son of God speaks, the Father listens and responds. Martha knew by faith whom to turn to when tragedy struck. Do you?

Tested by Fire

This is an important question, for we discover our true convictions when our faith is tested by fire. When tragedy strikes you, where do you turn? When you are filled with pain, where do you go?

This may seem to be a simple question with an obvious answer. "Of course," we say, "like Martha, I will turn to the Lord and His Word." May God grant that we will! But it is much easier to say this when life is good and problems are rare. When we are safely in the realm of the hypothetical, it is easy to be strong. We have no problem confessing our faith when death has not dealt us a crippling blow. But when times aren't so good, when death visits our family, we discover how weak we can really be.

We must grapple with the serious nature of our sinful condition before giving a trite answer. One has only to turn to the news reports to know that even Christians turn to many false sources of comfort. What Christian hasn't cringed when a well known preacher is in the news because of a sexual scandal, an affair, or for embezzlement? What believer has not grieved when he discovered a brother or sister in Christ has become snarled in drug or alcohol abuse?

Sin is real, and we all have real weaknesses. When you are hurting, where are you tempted to turn for comfort? Does pornography seduce you with its false promise? Does food lure you with a temporary satisfaction? Does the love of money draw you to possessions that end up possessing you?

These are important issues to deal with, for when someone we really love dies, part of us seems to die with them. We are no longer in a hypothetical situation; we are in real pain. And in our pain we desire comfort, healing, and life. There are many destructive behaviors which promise life, but they are false counselors. Their promises are empty—they cannot bring real life out of death, any more than you or I can raise the dead.

There is only one person who can bring us life—Jesus. Jesus said to Martha, *"Your brother will rise again."* In making such a promise, He was leading Martha to look for hope in the only place it could be found—in Him. Only Jesus can make such a bold statement in the face of death.

Do you remember how the apostle John, in verse 17, told us that Lazarus had been in the tomb for four days? Lazarus wasn't just a little bit dead—he was really dead! After four days, the physical signs of death in the body would be very obvious. After four days, the initial shock of death for the family would have begun turning into numbness and depression. The reality would have begun to sink in—Lazarus was really dead!

Into the midst of all this, Jesus strides into the family and says, *"Your brother will rise again."* Wow! That's bold!

The Resurrection Is a Person

And what a bold faith Martha expressed! Martha said to Him, "I know that he will rise again in the resurrection on the last day." In the face of her brother's death, Martha pointed her hope to the future, to a day when God would raise her brother from the dead. Despite her earthly loss, Martha kept her eyes focused on the life to come. God would bring a day of life, of resurrection.

Little did Martha know that she would get a preview of the resurrection day on the very day Jesus came to visit her. You see, Jesus had something very profound to reveal to Martha and to us.

"Jesus said to her, 'I am the resurrection and the life; he who believes in Me will live even if he dies, and everyone who lives and believes in Me will never die.'" [26]

When is the resurrection? That is the question before us. For Martha, the resurrection was a day that was still to come, when God will raise the bodies of the dead.

I suspect this is how we usually think of the resurrection as well. We wait for a day in the future, the resurrection of the dead, when our loved ones will be raised.

And while the Bible clearly teaches that this will happen some day, Jesus reveals that the resurrection is much more. He says, "*I am the resurrection and the life.*"

Jesus reveals that the resurrection is not a distant day in the future; the resurrection is a Person. Jesus makes it known that life is not a concept—He is life! Standing before Martha is Life in the flesh!

Consider what an awesome statement Jesus is making about Himself. There is no life without God, for God gave life from Himself and created all earthly life. "*In the beginning, God created the heavens and the earth.*" [27]

Without God, there are no heavens and no earth. Without God, there is no life in the universe. And there is no life for mankind without God, for it was the Lord who "*breathed into his nostrils the breath of life, and man became a living being.*" [28]

So when Jesus says, "*I am the resurrection and the life*," He is putting forth His claim that He is God in the flesh. He is saying that He is the source of life, that in His very flesh He carries the life of the entire universe.

So physical death is not a barrier to this One who is Life In The Flesh, who breathed the breath of life into the first man.

When Jesus shows up, life shows up. When Jesus comes onto the scene, the resurrection comes onto the scene.

That's why when Jesus returns at His second coming, the resurrection of the body will occur. The God who is life will give life to all.

So while Martha (and we) may talk in terms of an event, Jesus talks in terms of a person. For Martha, the resurrection was something that God would do someday. For Jesus, the resurrection is Himself.

What joy there is for us in this! Eternal life is not something we have to wait for. John writes about this in chapter 6 of his Gospel account: "*Truly, truly I say to you, he who believes has eternal life.*"[28] When God creates faith in your heart and you believe in Jesus, then He who is the resurrection and the life lives in you. Eternal life takes up residence in your heart! It isn't something that you have to wait for—it's already done. The resurrection of your body is something that will follow what has already happened—a resurrection in your heart!

Jesus has come to give life by creating this kind of faith. So after Jesus makes the profound statement that He is the resurrection and the life, He follows with a question to Martha: "*Do you believe this?*" He calls on Martha to trust His message, to put not only Lazarus' life in His hands, but also her own.

And that is what Jesus is looking to do for you. When we read the Bible, we are not simply reading ink on paper; we are reading the living words of God. When we hear the gospel of Jesus Christ proclaimed, we are not listening to a self-help message; we are experiencing God Himself at work creating eternal life in the hearts of people.

What joy Jesus must have felt when He heard Martha say, "Yes, indeed, Lord; I have believed that You are the Christ, the Son of God, the one who comes into the world." Martha had been given eternal life through faith in the Son of God. Jesus would soon reveal how true her faith was.

Jesus is looking to make a personal connection to you, if you do not know Him by faith already. He wants to give you the life that does not end, the life that is eternal.

And if, like Martha, you do know Him already, Jesus is looking to strengthen you for whatever might lie ahead. With Jesus in your heart and mind, you can face the tragedies of life—and death—with confidence, hope, and strength. And you can face your own death with faith, for Life Himself lives in you. You won't be facing death alone.

Chapter 8

If Only You Had Been Here

The doctors had given up. "There's nothing we can do," they said. "Fortunately, your condition isn't fatal. You'll just have to learn to live with it." And so she had. Year after year she had learned to deal with the pain. Year after year she had wondered why this had happened to her. Was God punishing her?

And then she had heard the rumors. There was a man they were saying who could heal her with just a touch. "A man of God," they were saying. But she was so afraid. Any man of God would be able to tell that she was unclean—the Bible said anyone with her kind of bleeding was unclean. But the Bible also told of prophets who could give God's healing with just a touch. If she could just touch His garment, she believed that God would heal her.

And so she approached Jesus as He was on His way to the house of Jairus. She reached out her hand, touched the hem of His garment, and she was healed! It was over! It was all over!

But it wasn't over. Jesus turned around in that noisy, jostling crowd of humanity and asked, *"Who touched me?"* How her heart must have been in her throat! "How could He know?" She looked at the ground nervously, fearing to make eye contact with Jesus, fearing that her unclean past would now haunt her present and her future. Still Jesus kept looking and asking. She knew that she had to come forward. Why was He making her do this? [30]

This woman trusted that just by touching the hem of His garment, she would be healed—and she was healed physically. But something more needed to be done. There was additional healing that she needed, healing that she may not have been aware of. This is why Jesus stopped. This is why Jesus asked, *"Who touched me?"* He knew who had touched Him. The Son of God knows when He heals someone. But He also knew that she needed an inner healing. The pain of her illness had been the lens through which she had seen life. She saw herself as diseased and deficient, as damaged goods. She saw herself as the Old Testament law pictured her, ritually unclean, unfit to go before God at His temple. [31] Perhaps she saw herself as many in her culture did—a sinner getting what she deserved. [32]

She needed a new perspective, a new way of looking at herself. She needed to see herself as God did—healed, restored, and loved. So Jesus took the time to call her out, so to speak. He waited, asking who touched Him, until she could stand it no more and revealed that she was the one. The Gospel of Mark tells us that she was trembling with fear when she fell at His feet. She had touched Him with her uncleanness—was Jesus angry? Jesus had made public her deed—would He now humiliate her before all these people? Would He speak out loud the shame that she felt inside? Would He call her "unclean," as she had been called, for so many years?

He would not. Jesus said, *"Daughter, your faith has healed you."* Astounding! He called her *"daughter"*! This woman saw herself as an unclean sinner before God, but God called her His daughter, even as He freed her from suffering. She had been lost in suffering and pain, but Jesus had found her!

Lost in Pain

That's the kind of Savior Jesus is—he is always looking for the person who is lost in suffering, pain, and sin. He is always ready to heal with a touch, to bring new hope and life.

In John 11:28, Jesus was looking for someone who was lost in a slightly different manner. Mary knew who Jesus was—he was her Lord and Savior. Yet she was still lost—lost in a grief that made her feel isolated and alone. Full of love and compassion, Jesus came looking for her.

> *"And after she had said this, she went back and called her sister Mary aside. 'The Teacher is here,' she said, 'and is asking for you.'"* [33]

We don't really know why Mary didn't come with Martha when Jesus first arrived (v. 20). For some reason, she decided to stay at home when Martha went to greet Jesus. I can imagine some of the possible reasons, because there have been times that I have avoided Jesus in the midst of my pain. When we are hurting, we often avoid the very One who can give us the greatest help. Why do we do that?

Disappointment is one reason. Mary loved Jesus, and she knew that He loved her family. Yet, when they needed Him the most, it seemed that He had failed them. He hadn't come in time to heal Lazarus, as she knew He could have. Her disappointment may have been so deep, her depression so strong, that she just couldn't bear to look Jesus in the eyes and talk to Him.

Has God disappointed you as you have wrestled with death? When your husband died, did your depression create a wall of numbness and shock that made it nearly impossible to pray? When your child was taken from you at an early age, were you so bitterly disappointed in God that you could not bear to worship Him because of the pain?

Fear is another reason we avoid God. Mary may have been afraid of the overwhelming emotions that stirred inside her. What if she couldn't control herself? What if she said things that were embarrassing or hurtful or blasphemous when she talked with Jesus? Better to stay at home and wait until she was able to control herself.

This is a very cunning and deceptive lie we tell ourselves. If we just wait long enough, we think, our emotions will subside and then we can be in control. The problem is that when we suppress our emotions, they don't go away, they just go down deep. I have known people over the years who have never dealt with the loss of a parent. It has kept them from a rich and full relationship with the Lord. What a waste!

There is another reason we avoid God—anger! Perhaps Mary was angry with Jesus—it happens. Maybe she couldn't understand why He didn't come, considering that He was practically family to them. Didn't that count for anything with Jesus?

Consider the statement that Martha made earlier and that Mary makes here. "*Lord, if you had been here, my brother would not have died.*" Ouch! It's as if Mary were saying, "If only you had been here, things would have turned out differently. Jesus, if you hadn't been so late, everything would have been okay." There's more than just a statement being made here, isn't there? This is an accusation. Along with these words comes a pointing finger, a finger pointed at the chest of Jesus. "Where were you when I needed you? It would have been so easy for you to come. Why didn't you?"

We are tempted to doubt God's love for us when we are in pain. When God doesn't live up to our expectations, we often become frustrated with Him. "What good is it to be a follower of Jesus if He isn't there for you when you need Him the most?" we think.

There are lots of reasons we avoid Jesus when death comes. The good news is that Jesus doesn't avoid us. "The Teacher is here, and is asking for you," Martha says to Mary. Jesus will not let Mary's pain be her burden alone. Jesus will not allow disappointment and depression to sweep over Mary like a tsunami bent on destruction. He is not going to abandon Mary to a prison made with the walls of her fear. Jesus is not afraid to face Mary's anger over her loss. He loves her. He looks for her. He calls on her to come to Him with her pain.

He Is with You!

Jesus comes looking for you when death has struck a painful blow. In our times of greatest need, Jesus comes looking for us. Into our disappointment and depression, Jesus comes. As our fears regarding death and sorrow put a noose around our lives, Jesus reaches in to cut those ropes. When anger and rage come billowing out of our hearts and mouths, Jesus stays with us, unafraid of our accusations, unyielding in His love for us.

So it's okay to come to Jesus and say, "I'm too depressed to pray." God will send people to pray with us and for us. Even better, the Holy Spirit prays for us with groans that are too deep for words to express. [34] It's okay to acknowledge our fears and let the emotions out in worship—Jesus and His people weep with us. It's okay for us to bring our questions to God. In fact, Jesus wants to hear them. Jesus comes looking for us even when we accuse Him of not being there for us, of not caring for us.

There is an old story about a theatrical presentation that sticks in my mind very clearly. The drama begins with a stage full of characters, milling about and talking all at once. It is impossible to make out what anyone is saying at first. Then, one character comes to the front and begins to speak loudly while the other characters quiet their voices. He is angry, for he has been physically beaten and abused. "It isn't fair for God to judge me!" he says. "Who does He think he is? I did nothing to deserve imprisonment and beatings! I'm an innocent man."

A second character approaches front and center, a young woman with a child. She also has a complaint. "My son and I have been discriminated against unfairly, simply because we are part of a minority ethnic group. We have often been forced to take the leftovers of those in power. We are invisible to some people and hated by others. What right does God have to judge me?"

Character after character shares stories of suffering and pain. Eventually, they all decide to put God on trial and a jury is selected. The charge? Failure to understand the human race. After hearing the evidence and deliberating over it, the jury finds God guilty. And the sentence is passed: God must be born under questionable circumstances into a minority. He must live in fear for His life even as a child. As an adult, He is to be poor, homeless, and not respected by those in power. Ultimately, He will be falsely arrested and unjustly imprisoned. He will be beaten and tortured, then finally executed, all for not understanding the human race.

While this sentence is being pronounced, a spotlight begins to shine on the back of the stage. It illuminates a picture of Jesus, the Son of God, hanging on a cross.

God understands the human experience, my friend. He understands how cruel people can be. He knows physical pain intimately. And He knows how it feels to take your last breath, to feel your final strength slip away.

That's the kind of Savior we have. He understands better than we do the weight of our sin, for He carried it to a cross. He understands the pain of death, for He died the death that we deserve.

So remember, when sin and death have done their worst, you have Someone looking for you. When death strikes a mortal blow to your heart, when your emotions seem to do whatever they want to do, remember that He is there for you. The Teacher is calling for you. You aren't alone in your pain.

Chapter 9

A Companion on the Road of Grief

In the movie Castaway, Tom Hanks portrays Chuck Nolan, a FedEx® employee who survives an airplane crash, only to be marooned on an island by himself for years. His ingenuity and resourcefulness help him to survive. He is able to find shelter, food, and water. But his ongoing problem is his loneliness. He has lost his job, his life, the woman he loved. It breaks his heart to be so alone.

Chuck has one companion: Wilson. Wilson is a volleyball which also survived the crash. Without any human companionship, Chuck makes a friend out of the ball. He paints a face on Wilson. He talks to Wilson, even argues with him. Wilson is his constant companion as he tries to ward off the depression and suicidal feelings he has in his loneliness. And when he is separated from Wilson at sea in his makeshift raft, he cries.

When you lose a member of your family, especially your spouse, the feelings of grief and loss are very intense. These feelings can make us feel marooned, alone, isolated. Yes, people can share food, shelter, and the basics with you. But very, very few people seem to be able to share your pain. Everyone else seems to go back to regular life, except you. Everyone else seems to be able to smile. But you wrestle with depression, month after month. Perhaps thoughts of suicide creep into the back of your mind. And maybe your best friend becomes a dog, a cat, or even a volleyball.

When death hurts us, we need help. We need a companion on the road of grief.

Solitary Confinement

Do you ever wonder if God understands your feelings? There have been times in my life where I was filled with grief because of one loss or another, and I struggled to put into words what my heart and soul were feeling. Let me give you an example.

My wife, Beth, has been a marvelous wife, friend, and support. When we were first married, we really enjoyed being together, going out with friends, being spontaneous. The freedom just to be with one another was exhilarating and so fulfilling. But we both had agreed before we were married that we wanted to have children. Beth earned a degree as an educator and has been a teacher in a number of primary age classrooms. I have spent many an hour with junior high students in Bible classes. Between the two of us, we had a strong desire to be parents.

But after a year of trying to conceive, nothing was happening. We began to be concerned, and talked to our doctor. I began to have some medical tests done, to see what the problem could be. It didn't take long to get the news. We wouldn't be able to biologically conceive a child.

And wouldn't you know, this happened just at the time we were moving. I had received and accepted a call to a new congregation. We got the medical news on a Monday and moved on the Wednesday of that same week. We moved away from Beth's brother, his wife, and their three sons, whom we were very close to. We moved away from a loving congregation with all of the support the body of Christ brings. And while we had met some of the people at our new church, we didn't have any close friends we could confide in.

So we were alone, and I was alone with the knowledge that I was unable to father a child. What a tremendous blow that was to us, and how guilty I felt! Intellectually, I knew that there was nothing I could do about it, yet I felt tremendous guilt over the fact that I could not father a child with my wife. I could not give her the son or daughter she longed for.

How can one adequately express those feelings? What could I say? For once in my life, I didn't have a lot to say. People who know me might chuckle—it seems I always have something to say. How odd for a pastor not to have words, right? But it happened to me and, I suspect, has happened to many of you. There are times we ourselves don't even know how to label or express the feelings that well up inside. If that is the case, we think, how can God possibly understand if we don't even know what we are feeling?

Perhaps you have walked down that lonely street, filled with feelings of loss, grief, or sorrow, yet find yourself unable to articulate them. You wonder how anyone could understand. You wonder if even God can understand.

Our Friend in Need

I have great news for you! Jesus does understand. And He understands not in a cold, intellectual manner, but in a very human, very vulnerable way.

Here at the tomb of Lazarus, as Mary falls at His feet weeping, as her friends join her in weeping, we are told in John 11:33 that Jesus was "deeply moved in spirit and troubled." Jesus saw and felt those powerful emotions of grief, not from a distance, but up close and personal. God was connecting to human grief.

In Jesus, God became flesh, John says. *"In the beginning was the Word, and the Word was with God, and the Word was God...The Word became flesh and made his dwelling among us."* [35] When Jesus was born, God bridged the gap between Himself and humanity that sin had created. Because Jesus walked on this earth, God knows the human experience first hand. Imagine that—God was born, just like you and me and everyone else. He grew up in diapers and learned to talk from His Mommy and Daddy, Mary and Joseph. Jesus became hungry and thirsty; He sometimes needed a nap because He was completely tired out. He was and is fully human.

As we read the Gospels further, we watch our God run the gamut of human emotions. Jesus became angry at His disciples when they kept the children from Him. He had compassion on the crowds who were harassed and helpless, like sheep without a shepherd. He experienced great joy when His disciples returned from their first mission trip. Jesus shares with us every human emotion, every high and low that comes with life.

Do you want to know what God is like? Then look at Jesus. Do you want to see if God cares? Then look at the Savior as He encounters people suffering from all kinds of things.

Here in John 11, God in the flesh shares Mary's sorrow. When He sees the grief that is pouring out of Mary's eyes and Mary's heart, it moves Him.

Our God is not distant. When you hurt, it matters to God because you matter to God. Your Savior understands your tears, your grief, and your fears. When you lose somebody, He feels that loss. When a family member dies, Jesus knows your hurt. When you cry into your pillow at night, unable to fathom the depth of your pain, Jesus knows. He is involved in your life. He shares your grief.

Get This Guy a Box of Tissues!

John 11:35 is famous as the shortest verse in the Bible. But it also should be famous because of what it tells us. Just look at what Jesus did in verse 35. He cried! This little verse has a big message. Jesus wept. The Son of God cried with His people over the pain death causes.

It is hard work, grieving with someone else. To spend an hour talking with someone who has just suffered a loss can be exhausting. Weeping with those who weep seems to take more energy than rejoicing with those who rejoice. Yet, here is Jesus, the man with the greatest burden of all, the salvation of humanity, sharing the burden of a woman in need.

It would have been easy to be superficial. Say a few appropriate words, make a show of sympathy, and get out of there. After all, Jesus had a bigger job, right? He had thousands of people who wanted a piece of His time. He was ushering in the Father's kingdom.

Yet Jesus remained authentic and genuine. This strongest of all men broke down and cried. Jesus was deeply moved. He not only saw the emotions of Mary and her friends, He felt His own.

Remember, verse 33 says that Jesus was "deeply moved in spirit and troubled." The Greek word here translated "troubled" is used of Jerusalem's turmoil over the announcement of a new king in Matthew 2:3. It describes the fearful emotional state of the disciples in Matthew 14:26 when they see what they think is a ghost walking on the water. It describes roiling water in John 5:7. Jesus' insides are churning as He experiences grief Himself. He has a gut-level reaction to what is going on, and He cries. What do these tears mean?

To the Jews who were watching, the tears of Jesus were the visible proof that He loved Lazarus. "See how He loved him!" they say in verse 36.

But their idea of love was the love of friendship. Do you remember how verse five of John 11 said that Jesus loved this family? The word used here by the Jews in verse 36 is a different word for love. They were talking about *filial* love, the kind of love between friends, the sort of love that might come naturally at the annual family reunion, the sort of love we might feel towards fellow golfers or fellow quilters, because we are in the same family or share the same hobby.

Now remember the kind of love Jesus has for His friends, the *agape* love we saw in verse 5. This is the sacrificial, unconditional love of God for His people that Jesus brought when the Son of God became man. The tears of Jesus expressed the *filial* love that Jesus had for His friends, to be sure. Because Jesus is fully human, He felt their pain as a friend or family member does. But the tears of Jesus also pointed to His *agape* love, the sacrificial love that led Him to show that love in a different, visible way—his death on a cross.

Jesus wept for Mary and Martha and Lazarus, but He also wept for a lost, suffering, and dying humanity. Jesus cried because He was their friend but also because He was their God. The Creator weeps for His lost creatures; the undying One weeps for those who must die.

So Jesus felt that tightness in the throat that you feel when the tears are about to come. Jesus felt the tears running down His face and tasted their saltiness in His mouth, just as you have. Perhaps He sobbed, His body shaking with the grief, just as you have wept.

Jesus knows what it feels like to cry. Jesus knows how it feels to stand at the cemetery and weep. He has done it. We have a Savior who shares our tears.

How important this is for us to remember! We are tempted to think that God doesn't love us when a loved one is injured in an accident or contracts a serious disease. And if that loved one dies, we may wonder why God didn't intervene, despite our fervent prayers.

Some of the people who gathered to grieve with Mary and Martha had those same thoughts. Notice what they say in verses 36–37.

"Then the Jews said, 'See how he loved him!' But some of them said, 'Could not he who opened the eyes of the blind man have kept this man from dying?'"

The Jews present to grieve with Mary couldn't reconcile their idea of love with the death of Lazarus. If Jesus really loved him, they reasoned, Jesus would have kept this man from dying. In essence, they were saying, "Jesus could have kept him from dying, but He didn't. What kind of love is this?"

Jesus did love this family. But Jesus loved them with a deeper kind of love, a love that prompted Him to give them more than they were asking for. Lazarus was allowed to die so that Jesus could reveal the life He gives, the life that does not end.

Jesus loves you and your family, too. However, this doesn't mean that all the difficult and painful things will be removed from your life. It does mean that in the midst of your pain, He will love you more than ever. And it does mean that He freely gives the kind of life that can never be taken away.

So when you are hurting, remember that little verse with the big message. Jesus wept. God is moved by our pain and sorrow. He shares our tears.

But God has even gone a step farther. He shares our graves. There was another time when a man was dying, and people spoke out. There was another occasion when Jesus was asked to prove who He was.

"'Let this Christ, this King of Israel, come down now from the cross, that we may see and believe.' Those crucified with him also heaped insults on him." [36]

As Jesus hung on the cross, those watching asked Him to save Himself. They didn't believe He was who He said He was. They wanted proof on their terms.

Jesus didn't prove Himself to their satisfaction that day. He stayed on the cross, showing the true depth of His love. This love had led Him to go to the tomb of Lazarus, where He would do a great miracle. But His love for a fallen humanity would also lead Him to go to His own borrowed tomb to do a greater miracle. Jesus shares not only our sorrows and our tears, He shares our graves. Consider this:

- Lazarus had been buried in a cave with a stone to close it— the tomb of Jesus also was a cave closed with a stone.
- Jesus would walk to the tomb of Lazarus—but His dead body would be carried to His grave.
- Jesus would call Lazarus out of his tomb—but Jesus' enemies would seal and guard His tomb.

So His tears were just the beginning. Jesus would take on our sin, our death, and our grave so that His life could empty our tombs. *"This is love: not that we loved God, but that he loved us, and gave his Son as an atoning sacrifice for our sins."* [37] The love of Jesus would take Him to the cross and to our graves.

There is a wonderful prayer in a burial service that I use. It begins like this:

Almighty God, by the death of your Son Jesus Christ you destroyed death, by His rest in the tomb you sanctified the graves of your saints, and by His glorious resurrection you brought life and immortality to light so that all who die in Him abide in peace and hope. [38]

"By His rest in the tomb you sanctified the graves of your saints," it says. Jesus' body spent time in the grave for you, and His body was raised for you. He has led the way through the grave to life eternal. So your grave is "sanctified," which means it is holy, set apart. When your body is laid in its resting place, it is set apart by God. The one who knows the number of hairs on your head surely knows of your death and burial. His love for you is greater than you know. *"Precious in the sight of the Lord is the death of his saints."*[39]

Jesus will stand with you and beside you through it all. He will even be at your deathbed and all the way to the grave. There is no place you can go that He won't follow. He is your companion on the road of grief.

Chapter 10

Take Away the Stone

All of the kids in my family loved our paternal grandfather. Our maternal grandfather had died when we were quite young, so we didn't know him very well. But Grandpa Sommer lived quite a bit longer, and we became close to him. Grandpa and Grandma Sommer lived on a little farm in rural Washington State. It wasn't very big, but to a city boy it seemed like a whole new world. There were cherry trees in the yard and raspberry bushes out back. Sometimes Grandpa would pasture some cows for a neighbor who didn't have room for all of his cattle. Rhubarb grew in the garden, and Grandma had a love of rhubarb pie and a love of serving it to us. Thank goodness for the sweet ice cream that helped us learn to like rhubarb pie!

We would often celebrate the Fourth of July with Grandpa and Grandma. We would make a weekend of it and go fishing with Grandpa at a nearby lake for little perch, bluegill, and maybe a trout or a catfish. We would bring our little aluminum boat, and rent another so all seven of us could be on the water. All of us kids wanted to go in Grandpa's boat, so we could fish with him. I was always jealous when my older sister or brother was given the favored spot in the boat with Grandpa.

Grandpa Sommer had fished for much of his life, and for fish a lot bigger than we were catching. So there were times that he would set the hook on a tiny bluegill as if he had hooked a monster steelhead or salmon. I can recall one little fish that took an airborne journey from the water on one side of the boat, over the top of our heads, and back into the water on the other side, as Grandpa enthusiastically battled this four-inch monster.

We usually went once a year to get sweet corn, too. The sweet corn that grows in the river valleys of Washington State is incredibly good, and we didn't want to miss out. We would drive to a local farm near Grandpa and Grandma's place and buy several large burlap sacks of corn. That was the easy part. The hard part came when we had to shuck all that corn. For several hours we boys would be out in Grandpa's old wooden shed with him, peeling ear after ear of corn, trying to get as much corn silk off as we could. Grandma, Mom and Dad, and my sister Cheryl would be inside, working just as hard to prepare the corn for freezing. They would blanch the ears in hot water, cut off the kernels, and put them into freezer containers. It was a hard day's work, but boy was it worth it during the winter when we had delicious sweet corn for dinner!

I had just finished my sophomore year of college when Grandpa died. It was early summer, a few weeks after school had let out for summer vacation. My summer job was painting houses with my former basketball coach, so every morning was an early morning. The phone rang early that day with the bad news that Grandpa had died. I vividly remember eating raisin bran that morning and can clearly recall my tears dripping into the cereal bowl.

Then came the day of the memorial service. We kids were older now, so the whole family wasn't going to be able to drive there in the same vehicle and at the same time. My parents wanted to arrive early, so they could be with Grandma well before the service. They also wanted to go to the funeral home so they could view Grandpa's body. They asked if any of us kids wanted to go along.

I did. For some reason I wanted to see Grandpa one more time, so I went to the funeral home. This was the first time that somebody I really cared about had died. I had been to funerals before, but this was different. This was Grandpa.

Viewing the body of my grandfather was unlike anything I had ever experienced before. This was death, face to face. The funeral home had done a good job making my grandfather look as normal as one can look. In a way, he simply looked as if he were asleep. But his skin color wasn't quite the same as when he had been alive. And of course, he wasn't moving or breathing.

The Stench of Death

I can understand why many people don't wish to go to viewings. It is something of an unnerving experience to see death up close and personal. I can only imagine the difficulty of serving in active duty in the military or in law enforcement, where death is not kept clean and neat and in a funeral home. No, we don't like to see death. And with good reason. Death reminds us of our sin. Death reminds us of our frailty. Death reminds us that those closest to us will not be with us forever on this earth, or we with them. And death reminds us that nobody lives forever, that our day, too, will come. Why would anyone want to open a tomb? Yet Jesus wanted to open the grave of Lazarus.

"Jesus, once more deeply moved, came to the tomb. It was a cave with a stone laid across the entrance. 'Take away the stone,' he said. 'But, Lord,' said Martha, the sister of the dead man, 'by this time there is a bad odor, for he has been there four days.'" [40]

Take away the stone? Open up the tomb? I don't think so. You just don't do that, especially, as Martha pointed out, when a corpse has been lying there for four days. It would be unthinkable to put the family through more trauma and suffering. To see what death and corruption was doing to a loved one's body was simply not a good idea.

In the society Jesus lived in, burial of the dead was done as quickly as possible in most cases. If someone died in the morning, the burial would take place that afternoon or evening. Only if someone died later in the day would the burial wait for the following day. The Jews of Jesus' day and the Israelites before them did not normally practice embalming, as the Egyptians did, with the notable exceptions of Jacob and Joseph.[41] Nor did the Jews practice cremation, as the Romans sometimes did. Typically, the body would be washed and then wrapped in clean linen cloths that were packed with spices, to mask the smell. The burial would take place very quickly, unless the person who died was worthy of great honor. Caves were often used for burial, rather than digging into the ground. Caves could be enlarged or cut out of rock, for use by family members as the years went by. A large stone could be rolled across the entrance, both to prevent the body from being disturbed and to keep the odor in.

Lack of burial was considered an ultimate insult and a disgrace reserved for the bitterest of enemies killed in battle. You can understand why burial happened quickly. But also consider this. Without refrigeration or embalming, the bodies would begin to decompose quickly. The odor of death would only increase with the passage of time, and the physical condition and appearance of the body would begin to break down.

Yet Jesus asked for the stone at Lazarus's tomb to be taken away. Those present must have sucked in their breath, wondering what Jesus was doing. Martha and Mary's friends probably held quiet conversations about what to do to avoid a real catastrophe. Jesus had gone over the edge. He was not acting in a rational manner. He was going to bring more grief and pain to this family with His crazy words and unrealistic promises.

But Jesus knew that the only way for Him to reveal life was to go into the stronghold of death and reveal the power He had over life and death.

I believe that this is one reason why God wants us to deal with death. Our only chance for life occurs when God opens our eyes to the fact that without Jesus, we are dead. We are conceived and born into sin, says Psalm 51:5. Ephesians 2:1–5 teaches us that we are, by nature, dead in our sins. And we are. Our bodies just take some time to catch up and die, but without Jesus, we are dead nonetheless.

In great mercy and love for us, Jesus wants us to see this essential truth. Think about it: Lazarus was really dead. He wasn't in a coma; he wasn't on life support; he was really, really dead. Four days dead, four days in the tomb. Jesus would show His power over death by giving life to a really dead man.

Get Real About Death

What are the gravestones in your life? I know of several people who have never been able to come to grips with the death of a loved one. One man is a husband, whose wife and kids are very faithful in worship. But his father and his wife's father died some years ago, and he hasn't been able to come to grips with the death of these well-loved men. And so he keeps the heavy stone of death over the doorway of his heart. It keeps a lid on his pain and hurt. He stays away from God, because that's risky. What if God asks him to open up? What might happen if those long-submerged feelings are allowed to surface?

Death does that to us sometimes. It makes us fearful and cautious, reluctant to share with God how hurt we are and how sad we feel. So we put that stone back over the emotional stench we fear. We keep it closed up, far away, protected.

Indeed, this is what our culture does with death. We live in a culture where we are so aware of death. Like never before, we are made aware of all the dying that goes on in this world. When we are at war, we get the daily report of how many soldiers have died. We often are even told how they died. In every edition of the evening news, we are told who was killed in an accident, who was murdered, and who was killed in a natural disaster. Oh, yes, our culture is very aware of death as it happens. Yet that same culture often does its very best to avoid the unpleasant reality of death.

Years ago, I went to a funeral home to comfort a family as they went to the viewing of their loved one. A very interesting choice had been made for the viewing. The body of the deceased person was not lying in a casket, but was in a bed with the covers drawn up, just as if he had been taking a nap.

Death is more than falling asleep. Although Jesus Himself refers to the death of Lazarus as "falling asleep," He does so to highlight His ability to wake someone up at the resurrection, not to give the impression that death is any less severe. You see, the Bible speaks very clearly about death—it is the result of sin: *The wages of sin is death.* [42]

Our culture does not want to speak of this. Have you ever noticed that whenever a funeral is held, especially for someone famous or notable, that we all tend to say only the very best things about the person who died? We always talk about how much she loved her family. We make sure to mention how hard he worked to make others happy. You <u>don't</u> hear at a funeral; "Joe was really kind of a bad guy. He got what he deserved." People don't say at a memorial service "Kim didn't really love her family that much."

Yet the Bible is absolutely clear on this matter. In Matthew 5:48, Jesus said, *"Be perfect, therefore, as your heavenly Father is perfect."* He also said, *"No one is good but God alone."* [43] The reason we have funerals is because we aren't good by God's standard of perfection. Our sinful nature and rebellion is the cause of our deaths. We are dead and it is our own doing. That's not something that people are saying much these days. People want to leave the door of the grave closed. Our sinful nature doesn't want us to accept responsibility for sin and death. So we cover it up. We make it look nice. We say nice platitudes when someone dies.

Opening the Casket

Jesus comes along and says, *"Take away the stone."* In other words, He says, *"Let's be real about this. And don't worry about the smell of death—I have a remedy for that: sweet smelling life."*

> *"'But, Lord,' said Martha, the sister of the dead man, 'by this time there is a bad odor, for he has been there four days.' Then Jesus said, 'Did I not tell you that if you believed, you would see the glory of God?' So they took away the stone."* [44]

What a dramatic moment this must have been for everyone gathered at the tomb of Lazarus! And what an act of faith for Martha and her sister! Every thing that they had ever observed in their lives told them that death was permanent. As little girls, when their pet dog died, that was it. He was gone. When their grandparents and uncles and aunts had breathed their last, life was over and done with.

Every fiber of their being and every thought of their minds must have wanted so desperately to keep that stone over the entrance into the grave. They didn't want to look at death again.

But walking by faith and not by their sight, they listened to the words of Jesus. The promises of Jesus outweighed their life experiences. The words of Jesus were stronger than their rational thought processes. The living Word of God in the flesh, standing next to them, spoke a stronger language than the words of their logic and emotions. So they took away the stone.

You and I live in a world that still operates much as it did in Martha and Mary's day. When your dog dies, it stays dead. When your grandfather breathes his last, he does not return. All of our experience, all of our science tells us that when a person dies, that is the end of it all. But we don't want to lose life. We want to exist, we want to feel, we want to live! This is one reason we fear death so much—it seems so permanent.

Jesus, however, calls on us to listen to His Words above all else. He wants us to walk by faith in Him, not by our limited sight. That is why a Christian memorial service features the words and promises of the Savior, more than it highlights how "good" someone was. It is the promise of the gospel, the good news of Jesus risen from the grave, which gives life to us now and will give life eternal to our new, improved bodies someday.

"*Take away the stone*," Jesus says. Caskets and cemeteries and graves hold death in. They are places for the bodies of those who have died. They are also places which hold our greatest fears. Let me share a real life example.

It was just a matter of going through the door. It was something she had done thousands of times in her life. You walk across the room to the doorway and go through. A very kind and thoughtful man was even holding the door open for her. It couldn't be any easier! Yet, she couldn't go through that door. I know because I was with her. I was standing beside this dear lady, holding her hand, encouraging her. Yet when we came to that doorway, she physically could not move for about thirty seconds!

Why was she having problems? This daughter of the Lord was standing outside the door of a room at the funeral home. She and I had met in a smaller, more comfortable room with the funeral director. We had gone over the details of a memorial service for her husband, who had unexpectedly died just a few days earlier. She had done very well as we talked about what kind of a burial she wanted, the costs involved and the things she had to do. Everything had been finished except for one painful task. She had to choose a casket for the body of her husband.

This was the room that was difficult to enter—the casket room. As we walked toward that room, the funeral director opened the door. Her hand began to tremble as she saw twenty or thirty caskets set up in the room. Some were ornate, expensively designed. Others were more simple and modest. But all of them were open. All of them were mute reminders that her husband was gone, that death had unexpectedly shattered her life. And she couldn't move. These caskets were inescapable visuals, unavoidable signs that death was real, that death had taken someone she loved away from her.

We fear the sights of death. We don't like to go into a funeral home or visit the cemetery. We push these things away; we close the doors of our minds and hearts to this fearful thing known as death. The door of the grave is a fearful thing to open.

The Grand Opening

Jesus wants us to remember that the grave really is an open door. In John 14:2–3, Jesus speaks some very comforting words.

"In my Father's house are many rooms; if it were not so, I would have told you. I am going there to prepare a place for you. And if I go and prepare a place for you, I will come back and take you to be with me that you also may be where I am."

The journey to the Father's house led to a cross and then to the grave. For Jesus to give us life, He Himself had to experience death and the grave. But death couldn't hold on to Him. I just love the description Matthew gives about the tomb in his resurrection account:

"There was a violent earthquake, for an angel of the Lord came down from heaven and, going to the tomb, rolled back the stone and sat on it." [45]

The stone in front of Jesus' tomb appeared to be a grim reminder that Jesus had lost and His enemies had won. It seemed to show that death swallows all the living. But for an angel, it was a chair to sit on! An angel of the Lord rolled that stone away and sat on this symbol of death!

Talk about a Grand Opening! In His resurrection, Jesus has opened up the door to life for us. Because He has gone through death and the grave and has risen to prepare a place in His Father's house, the grave is a doorway to eternal life.

We were therefore buried with him through baptism into death in order that, just as Christ was raised from the dead through the glory of the Father, we too may live a new life. If we have been united with him like this in his death, we will certainly also be united with him in his resurrection. [46]

His death was yours—and His resurrection is yours as well! So you will follow Him through your grave to your resurrection.

Going through the door of your death will not be easy. But it is not the end. Jesus came to open Lazarus's tomb, and He will open yours. *"Take away the stone,"* Jesus will say. And death won't be able to hold on to you, any more than it could hold on to your Savior.

Chapter 11

Thankful in the Midst of Death?

Do you remember when you were in school and you knew the answer to a question the teacher had asked? Maybe you were used to answering a lot of questions in class. Perhaps you hardly ever raised your hand. Either way, when you knew the answer, you wanted to speak, because you knew you had it right. I had an experience a little bit like that on a game show.

A game show? Yes, I was on Wheel of Fortune® a few years ago. It was quite an experience, something that I won't forget for a while. We arrived at 9:00 am and were there past 5:00 pm. Most of our time was spent sitting around, listening to rules, procedures, and the like. But the game itself was a lot of fun. During the course of a round, word puzzles are put up on the board, letters are guessed, and contestants try to figure out what the words are.

A point comes during the round when somebody figures out what the answer is. During one of the rounds, I figured out the puzzle while the other two contestants were still taking their turns. Let me tell you, waiting for my turn was almost unbearable. I had the answer! I knew what it was! And I couldn't wait to give the answer, to shout it out! I had great joy when I was able to solve the puzzle.

Jesus Knows the Answer!

Jesus stood at the tomb of Lazarus, with the stone rolled away. Inside that tomb was a man dead for four days. Outside the tomb were grieving sisters, family members, and friends. Death surrounded them all. It was a hopeless situation, it seemed, with no happy solution. How can you figure out death? How does one see life in the midst of death?

Jesus knew the answer to this puzzle: God had created life, God sustains life, and God can give life to the dead. That is why in verse 41, Jesus began by thanking His Father. *"Father, I thank you that you have heard me."*

Who would possibly begin a prayer at a cemetery with words like that? One would expect beginnings like, "Father, we come to you in our time of grief," or "Father, we don't always understand why bad things have to happen." But Jesus began with a prayer of thanks. He prayed with confidence and trust in His Father.

That is why I think Jesus felt joy and excitement as He prayed in front of Lazarus' tomb. Something big was about to happen.

Jesus had joy and excitement, like I did on Wheel of Fortune®. But there is one major difference. My enthusiasm was based on what I might be able to win for myself. I was hoping to beat out my competition. I knew the answer and wanted to use that answer to get what I could for myself.

Can you imagine a contestant on a game show sharing the answer with a competitor? Can you imagine a contestant giving away an answer so that his competitor would win? That would never happen, because all of us would want to win and claim the prize for ourselves. But Jesus is different. The joy and excitement of Jesus comes not from what He might gain for Himself, but from what He might give to others. Instead of seeking to be served, Jesus came to serve. Instead of seeking a comfortable life for Himself, Jesus chose the way of the cross for our benefit. We were the prize He was seeking; we were the joy set before Him!

You Are a Visual Aid

Jesus knew the answer to the death of Lazarus was the life that was in Himself. What joy and anticipation must have filled His heart as He thought of giving Lazarus back to Martha and Mary! But Jesus had more in mind for this miracle.

"Father, I thank you that you have heard me. I knew that you always hear me, but I said this for the benefit of the people standing here, that they may believe that you sent me." [47]

The joy of Jesus comes from giving many people life, eternal life. His goal, His joy and excitement, was to create faith in the people who saw this miracle. Lazarus would be the visual aid Jesus would use to show the people who He was. In a way, by raising Lazarus, Jesus was saying, "Do you see how I gave him life? Believe that I am the one sent from the Father, and I will give all of you eternal life."

Jesus was showing that He is our connection to the Creator. The One who made all things good in the very beginning was in the process of making a new start in His Son. In the raising of Lazarus, Jesus was revealing this new start. Lazarus was not the center of this story, Jesus was. Lazarus was the visual aid to faith. When Jesus raised him from the dead, He wanted to make it clear that we have hope as we face death. In the Savior, humanity has a connection to the Father, the Creator of the Universe, the Giver of Life.

Jesus wants to share His gift of life with dying people like us. He has all the answers, even the answer to the grave. And so He prays a prayer of thanksgiving to His Father, for the benefit of those around Him that they might hear and believe.

Are you listening to Jesus? Do you hear the call to faith that Jesus gives you? Do you see what's going on here? Remember, Lazarus is the visual aid, Jesus is the focus. Jesus raised Lazarus so you might see who the giver of life is. Jesus brought this man out of the grave so that He might bring you out of your sin. He wants to give you faith in Him.

But this is about more than you and Jesus. This story is bigger than you and me. Jesus is still in the business of bringing new life through faith to people who are physically and spiritually dying without Him. He continues to have a bold and different message to give to the people of our postmodern world.

This is one of the reasons we have memorial services when a follower of Jesus dies. At these services, we boldly and joyfully thank God. We say things that don't make sense to those without Jesus. When a believer dies, we say, "Thank you Father, for listening to your children. Thank you for giving faith in Jesus and forgiveness of sins to our departed loved one. Thank you for the peace and joy you give us today and will give us in the days to come."

While there is real grief at a Christian burial, that grief is accompanied by hope. This is no false hope in human goodness. This is real joy, real peace, and real hope in our Savior. Jesus has given us life through faith in Him—why not be thankful, even as Jesus was thankful at the tomb of Lazarus?

This is one of the biggest reasons for us to have public memorial services. There are many people who don't want to enter a Christian worship service. They might be afraid of what they will hear. They may be angry over a past hurt. They might even believe that they have no need for God. Yes, many of these people won't come on a Sunday, or any other day, for that matter.

But if you have been a good friend to them, if you have shown them the care and love of Jesus, then they will come to your memorial service. They will enter a worship service and hear the message of God that they so desperately need. They will know the consequences of sin because of your death, but they will also hear the result of the gospel, the good news of the life Jesus has given you.

This is why we have Christian memorial services and Christian burials—not just for fellow believers, but for those who are physically living yet spiritually dead. We have these services so that believers might be comforted and non-believers might be converted. Remember, it wasn't about Lazarus—it's not going to be about you or me. It's always about Jesus.

Jesus has the answer to the biggest question of all—what do we do about death? In His death and resurrection, He won the contest, but He gives the prize to us. Life is given to us instead of death.

Jesus is excited to share this answer with many people. So take some time, sit down with your pastor, and plan a memorial service that will glorify God, and put your Savior front and center. And be thankful that, like Lazarus, you can be a visual aid that Jesus will use to bring people to eternal life.

Chapter 12

Lazarus, Come Out!

About five years ago I was involved in an accident on a highway not too far from where we live. I was driving home a few hours after lunch, and the afternoon traffic was beginning to swell, as it does every day. The traffic would go the speed limit for a while, and then would suddenly slow down in spots where there was congestion.

It was at one of these congestion spots that the accident occurred. I was in the fast lane, hoping to beat most of the traffic home, zipping along as I went. Suddenly, all the cars in front of me hit their brakes and abruptly came to a stop. I braked as hard as I could. For a few seconds I feared that I might hit the vehicle in front of me. Fortunately, I stopped a few feet from the rear bumper. "Whew!" I thought. "Just in time."

It was at that moment that I looked in the rear-view mirror and saw a large SUV coming at me. I knew there was no way he could stop in time. I couldn't take my eyes off the image in my mirror. The image of the front grill of this vehicle was getting larger and larger.

Bam! He shot into me, instantly knocking my car into the car in front of me. I felt my head whip back into the headrest and then forward again. A second car slammed into the vehicle behind me, giving me a second jolt. And then it was over.

In all, five or six cars were involved in the accident. Fortunately, no one was seriously injured, although most of our cars suffered pretty extensive damage. Although I was able to drive our car away, the damage to it was such that it was not repaired.

It was a funny feeling, sitting in my car, watching the vehicle behind me, knowing that there was going to be a collision. There was nothing I could do about it, even though I knew it was coming. And after the accident, after we had all gotten out to make sure no one was seriously hurt, I sat down again in my car and thought, "Now what? How are going to get out of here?" Our damaged cars were in the left lane of a four-lane highway. Cars were whizzing past us on the right. There was no way to get across with a damaged car. What would we do?

Thank God for the Highway Patrol! Within a few minutes, a black and white unit pulled up, with lights flashing. The uniformed officer was professional, yet courteous. He instantly sized up the situation and took action. First, he made sure no one was seriously hurt. Then, he checked with each of us to see how badly the various vehicles were damaged. One car had to be towed over to the side. The rest of us, he instructed, were to follow the tow truck, so that all the cars would be safely on the right shoulder of the highway. "Right," I thought. "How are we going to get across this busy highway?"

It was actually very easy. The officer walked to the back edge of the accident, close to the oncoming traffic. He held up his hand to stop the oncoming lanes. And sure enough, they stopped. As the approaching drivers saw the man with the badge and the uniform, when they observed his car and flashing lights, they knew he had the authority to stop the traffic. And so they brought their cars to a stop. Four lanes of highway traffic halted simply because the right man held up his hand. We crossed over to the shoulder without incident. This officer had the authority to do his job.

Lazarus had seen death coming. As he looked in the rear-view mirror of his life, Lazarus knew that this was it. His time had come. There was nothing that he or Martha or Mary could say or do that would change this fact. And death slammed into this family like a speeding SUV, breaking their hearts, crushing their hopes. Mary and Martha would drive away from this collision with death, but the damage to their hearts was done. They would never be the same again.

There is nothing you and I can say or do that can alter or reverse death. This is one of the things that is so frightening about death. We are completely out of control, unable to do anything to help ourselves or a loved one when death occurs. We are helpless to stop it. But Jesus is not.

Swapping Life for Death

As Jesus stood before the tomb of Lazarus, He called out in a loud and strong voice, *"Lazarus, come out!"* Notice that Jesus spoke in the imperative: He gave a command. He did not make a request; He gave an order. He didn't beg for help, He declared what was going to happen. The One who spoke the creation into being, the One who said, *"Let there be light,"* now spoke to the dead and said, *"Let there be life!"*

Only God can speak to the dead in this way. Only God has this kind of authority over death. The Son of God didn't come to stop traffic; He came to stop death dead in its tracks. He spoke to a dead man in order to give him life.

Have you heard His voice speaking to you? It's the most important message you could ever hear. Life is going to throw its accidents at you. Some of them are easier to recover from than others. But ultimately, in your rear-view mirror, you will see death approaching. You may have a long time to contemplate this, as a slow moving disease gives you time to ponder your mortality. Or you may have only a few seconds, as an accident or heart attack reveals that death has arrived.

Whatever forms our deaths may take, it is the voice of Jesus that rides high and clear above the noise and confusion. It is the living Word of God that speaks to our greatest weakness and makes us strong with His life, even when we are dying. For even the dead have to listen when Jesus speaks.

"The dead man came out, his hands and feet wrapped with strips of linen, and a cloth around his face. Jesus said to them, 'Take off the grave clothes and let him go.'" [48]

I must confess that the translation above is not my favorite, for it describes Lazarus as "the dead man". A better translation would probably be "the one who had died". You see, Lazarus had died, but he was dead no longer. He had all the markings of burial on him—his hands and feet were wrapped, and there was a cloth around his face. But he was alive! This man who had been dead was now raised to life! What an incredible miracle! Consider what this means for all believers!

- Even death must bow down to the Lord of life.
- Sin meets its match in the Lamb of God, who dies to permanently remove our sin.
- The curse of our mortality, placed upon humanity when paradise was lost, is lifted away when Jesus speaks life into the dead.

Jesus now directed the people to unbind Lazarus and let him go. The trappings of death and burial, the wrappings, the cloth around his face, the spices, all of it was to come off. Lazarus was free to go, to live! Can you imagine what this must have been like?

People had to have been beside themselves with joy, wonder, and amazement. What a celebration Mary and Martha must have had! What a joy and tear-filled reunion they must have had with their brother! He was alive!

I wonder what Jesus was thinking at this moment. He alone, of everyone there, understood the price that must be paid for this raising from the dead. Only He could fully understand what it would cost to bring life to spiritually dead and physically dying people. He had to die.

As they took off the grave clothes that had been on Lazarus, did Jesus think of how His body would be similarly wrapped? As they unbound the hands and feet of His friend, did Jesus consider how spikes would go through His own hands and feet?

The price for bringing dead people like us out of death was the life of the Son of God. As we will see in just a few verses, the raising of Lazarus by Jesus was the final straw for His enemies. They would now put into action their plans to kill Him. Jesus knew full well what the cost of His ministry would be. But because He loves you and me so much, He was willing to face a brutal execution. He was willing to be put into a grave so that he could bring us out of our graves.

When Jesus died, a wealthy man named Joseph, along with a Pharisee named Nicodemus, wrapped the body of Jesus in a linen cloth and linen wrappings. They applied some spices to His body. Then a stone was rolled across the opening of the tomb, to seal it shut.[49]

Isn't that ironic? Jesus would put on grave clothes so that Lazarus could remove his. Jesus died in order to give life to him and to us. Our grave clothes have been removed, just like Lazarus. Because Jesus put on grave clothes and defeated death, we live clothed in a robe of life that will last forever. Because Jesus shed His grave clothes on Easter morning, we won't have to wear the trappings of the grave forever.

Harvest Time

In 1 Corinthians 15:20, we are told that *"Christ has indeed been raised from the dead, the firstfruits of those who have fallen asleep."* He is the first because His resurrection makes our resurrections possible. He is first, but He will not be the last.

We have an apricot tree in our front yard. I'm not much of a gardener, but despite me, that tree produces wonderful apricots about every other year. My daughter is especially eager to eat that delicious fruit, so it's hard for her to wait. "When will they be ripe, Daddy?" she asks. It seems there is always one, usually near the top of the tree, which gets ripe first. When that happens, we know that the other apricots are about to get ripe. It's just a matter of time. I can assure her that we will all be enjoying a wonderful harvest of fruit very soon.

Jesus is the firstfruits of the resurrection. His resurrection is the guarantee that ours will follow soon; it's just a matter of time. And what a harvest that will be!

A day will come, my friends, the day of the resurrection of all flesh, when the Lord of life will call all of our names and give us new bodies. Just listen to what the Lord promises us in His Word:

But your dead will live; their bodies will rise.

Isaiah 26:19

For my Father's will is that everyone who looks to the Son and believes in him shall have eternal life, and I will raise him up at the last day.

John 6:40

The creation itself will be liberated from its bondage to decay and brought into the glorious freedom of the children of God.

Romans 8:21

By his power God raised the Lord from the dead, and he will raise us also.

1 Corinthians 6:14

But our citizenship is in heaven. And we eagerly await a Savior from there, the Lord Jesus Christ, who, by the power that enables him to bring everything under his control, will transform our lowly bodies so that they will be like his glorious body.

Philippians 3:20–21

The Fashion Show of Life

When this marvelous day comes, all the trappings of death will be gone. Even as Lazarus was freed from the wrappings and the cloth around his face, we will be freed from coffins and cremations, from cemeteries and funerals, forever and ever. Can you imagine what that will be like? You will never again have to worry about your parents growing older. No one will talk about disease, because there won't be any. Cancer, HIV, SIDS, tuberculosis—they will all be gone. Your family will never make a visit to a grave again, and there will be no cemeteries or funeral homes. We won't ever attend a memorial service or a funeral. No one will feel that awful, permanent pain of separation that death brings. We will take off the grave clothes forever and be clothed in the righteous life of Jesus Christ for eternity. That gets me wound up just thinking about it!

But for now we have to wait, for *"the Lord is patient, not wanting anyone to perish."* [50] Waiting is hard to do sometimes. But while we wait, while we eagerly look forward to the resurrection, we aren't here just to sit around. Here on this earth, we have something to do, something of a dress rehearsal for the resurrection. In a way, we get to be like Lazarus and live without our grave clothes in this life also. We are putting on God's fashion show of life.

Have you ever wondered what Lazarus had to say when he came out of the tomb? The Bible doesn't tell us—and man, I wish it did! I would love to know what Lazarus talked about! Did he remember what had happened to him after his death? Could he describe heaven? Or was it so much beyond human understanding that he just couldn't put it into words? (The Apostle Paul describes such an experience in 2 Corinthians 12:1–4.)

If Lazarus was able to remember, I wonder if he wanted to return to where he had been. For as wonderful as earthly life can be, it is also full of thorns and thistles, trouble and heartache, and, ultimately, death. Lazarus had been removed from all those effects of our sin, yet the Lord called him back to life on this earth. Why?

Jesus needed to use him as a visual aid, a model of what He had come to do. The Lord of life wanted Lazarus to point others to the life he had been given in the Messiah. Lazarus could live without the fear of death because he knew where he was going. He knew what it was like to have the grave clothes taken off. He was living proof that the life Jesus gives cannot be taken away, even by death.

Our lives are also intended by God to be visual aids for others. We, too, are living proof of the eternal life Jesus gives now and forever. As I mentioned earlier, when a person receives God's gift of salvation by faith, he or she already has eternal life. Even though we have to wait for our bodies to be raised, we don't have to wait for God's gift of life everlasting. And so, in a sense, we can already shed our grave clothes. We can shed the grave clothes of the anxious fear of death. We can shed the grave clothes of hopeless grief when someone dies. We can be at peace with our mortality, knowing that God has won the ultimate victory in the resurrection of Jesus.

That is powerful in a world that struggles to deal with death. When you speak of God's gift of life and what it means to you in the midst of your grief, that witness has power. When you are able to face the death of your husband with hope, because he is a believer in the Son of God, God works powerfully through you. And when you are able to come to grips with your own death because Jesus has given you eternal life, this may be the most effective witness you could ever give!

Lazarus was unbound, free to live without fear of death, even though he would face death once more. For Jesus had revealed in Lazarus that death could not hold on to God's people. Lazarus was a model of what Jesus had come to do. And so are we. We are the models for God's fashion show of life. We don't have to be bound by our fears of the grave because we have been raised with Christ. We have had our grave clothes taken off. We are free to really live, free to share with others the life Jesus gives!

Chapter 13

A Matter of Life and Death

Abraham Lincoln was a man with strong character under pressure. Perhaps more than anyone else, Lincoln is a man who has shaped our nation. He was determined to hold the nation together. Even when the war was going badly for the North, when many people on both sides thought that two nations would surely be formed, perhaps should be formed, he remained constant. He would stand against slavery, which angered many, yet others were convinced he didn't move quickly enough to abolish slavery. One of the things I admire most about Abraham Lincoln is the fact that he believed in himself when very few others did. In 1863, there were many even *in the North* who wanted him to resign.

Francis Fisher Browne, in *The Every-day Life of Abraham Lincoln*, wrote of the opposition and difficulties Lincoln faced:

"So far had this gone, that early in 1863 we find Mr. Greeley searching everywhere for a fitting successor to Mr. Lincoln for the Presidency. There were but few men in high official station in Washington who at that time unqualifiedly sustained him." [51]

Yet Lincoln carried on. Why? Because he believed that he was doing the right thing. He believed that God had a job for him to do. And he would do that job, though he paid the ultimate price for following through.

It is in times of great trial and pressure that character is truly revealed. We only have to look at ourselves to know this is true. When great pressure is given to us at our jobs, how do we respond? When the kids intentionally argue and irritate each other, how long does your patience last? When you are stuck in traffic and are late for a meeting, what words enter your mind and exit your mouth?

The raising of Lazarus says a lot about the character and identity of Jesus. Jesus faced severe opposition from those who should have supported Him the most—the religious and political leaders of Israel. They had attempted to arrest Him before. The death of Jesus' relative, John the Baptizer, revealed how serious the danger was. Yet Jesus continued to be about His Heavenly Father's work. He would do His Father's will, even though it would cost Him dearly.

Who Is This Guy?

So Jesus raised Lazarus from the dead. Not only does this reveal Jesus' character of mercy, life, and love, it clearly points to the identity of Jesus. Old Testament prophecy speaks of what it would be like when the Messiah came. For example, the book of Isaiah says that He would be born of a virgin. [52] The prophet Micah adds that the Messiah would be born in Bethlehem. [53] But one of the references I love the most is found in Isaiah 35:3–6.

> *Strengthen the feeble hands, steady the knees that give way; say to those with fearful hearts, "Be strong, do not fear; your God will come, he will come with vengeance; with divine retribution he will come to save you." Then will the eyes of the blind be opened and the ears of the deaf unstopped. Then will the lame leap like a deer, and the mute tongue shout for joy. Water will gush forth in the wilderness and streams in the desert.*

When God would come, writes Isaiah, the blind would see, the deaf would hear, the lame would walk, and the mute person would talk. And this is exactly what Jesus did. This is partly what made Him so popular—he was helping so many people.

But He was more than a miraculous healer. Remember, these were signs that <u>God</u> had come to be with His people. And Jesus did more. He demonstrated the ability to command and control the forces of nature when He calmed the Lake of Galilee. He revealed His divine power over Satan by casting out demons from many people. Finally, Jesus showed His authority over life and death by raising the dead.

Death was the last arena of conflict, the ultimate battle where Jesus would reveal His identity. There are some prophetic passages in the Old Testament that are very pertinent to death and resurrection. Three verses: Psalm 49:15, Psalm 71:20, and Hosea 13:14 all ascribe to God the ability to raise the dead.

"But God will redeem my life from the grave; he will surely take me to himself."

Psalm 49:15

"Though you have made me see troubles, many and bitter, you will restore my life again; from the depths of the earth you will again bring me up."

Psalm 71:20

"I will ransom them from the power of the grave; I will redeem them from death. Where, O death, are your plagues? Where, O grave, is your destruction?"

Hosea 13:14

Jesus revealed who He was by fulfilling the prophecies of the Hebrew Scripture. His actions revealed that He was the long awaited Messiah. God had come to be with His people, bringing the Kingdom of Heaven. The New Testament takes that theme and runs with it, bearing clear witness to the identity of Jesus. He is the Son of God, come in the flesh, to give life to a humanity held in the icy grip of death.

This is not the Jesus of our popular culture, ready to give us self-help suggestions whenever we decide it's convenient. This is not the Jesus of other cults and religions, who picture Him as a prophet. This is not the Jesus of liberal theology, who is just a man with an important ethical message.

This is the historical Jesus of the Bible, showing you who He really is as He brings life out of death. He may not be who the world wants Him to be, but He is who the world needs. He is good news for a world filled with death. In Jesus, the Messiah, God comes to a world that is dying and offers life.

Letting Go So You Can Live

This is the good news Jesus showed when He raised Lazarus. And for many people that day, it made all the difference in the world.

"Therefore many of the Jews who had come to visit Mary, and had seen what Jesus did, put their faith in him." [54]

That word "therefore" is a big word. Mary's friends had come to help her grieve and to be with her in her time of need. But they experienced something that went far beyond their expectations. They saw Jesus fulfilling the Old Testament prophecies about the Messiah. They saw Jesus raising the dead. Therefore, many of them put their trust in Him.

But that wasn't the only reaction. As hard as it might be for us to understand, there were those who did not react positively to this miracle. They wanted to get rid of Jesus.

Then the chief priests and the Pharisees called a meeting of the Sanhedrin. "What are we accomplishing?" they asked. "Here is this man performing many miraculous signs. If we let him go on like this, everyone will believe in him, and then the Romans will come and take away both our place and our nation." [55]

Why? What reason could anyone possibly have for wanting to destroy someone who brought life? Why in the world would anyone want to kill Jesus, when He showed that He was the long awaited Messiah, ready to take on death?

The members of the Sanhedrin, the Jewish ruling council, could see the writing on the wall in the actions and words of Jesus. He was bringing a new way of life, what He called the Kingdom of God. They were very afraid of what might happen if Jesus continued on this course. If Jesus grew in popularity and influence, if He became the leader of all Israel, then their position of leadership would be ruined, as far as they were concerned. Their power and position was threatened by Jesus. They also saw in Jesus a threat to the very existence of Israel. They believed that the Romans would view Jesus as a dangerous leader who would lead the Jewish nation to rebel against Rome. They feared that Roman armies would come destroy Jerusalem, and Israel as a nation might cease to exist.

Sadly, while many Jewish people loved Jesus, the bulk of Jewish leadership saw Him as a dangerous threat to their power and their position. So, their reaction to this miracle was to set in motion their plans to have Him killed.

> *Then one of them, named Caiaphas, who was high priest that year, spoke up, "You know nothing at all! You do not realize that it is better for you that one man die for the people than that the whole nation perish." He did not say this on his own, but as high priest that year he prophesied that Jesus would die for the Jewish nation, and not only for that nation but also for the scattered children of God, to bring them together and make them one. So from that day on they plotted to take his life.* [56]

In a sense, Jesus *was* a threat to these men. By raising Lazarus from the dead, He was showing them (and us) that true life is found only in Him. Human concepts of power and position are nothing compared to the life Jesus brings. Jesus called on the leaders of the Sanhedrin to give up their efforts to hang onto the power they thought they had. He wanted them to see that leadership was an act of service, that leaders were put in place by God to serve those they lead.

This was the kind of leadership Jesus practiced, as He came not to be served but to serve.[57] Jesus really *was* a threat to the place of these leaders. He *did* want them to die to their pride, to their desire to wield power over others. He wanted them to serve God by putting their sinful and selfish natures to death and by serving others. Their response? They wanted Him to die.

Make no mistake about it. Jesus wants us to understand that we are like Lazarus. We have no life without Him. So He wants us to put to death all of our efforts to hang on to what we think is our life: prestige, power, money, comfort, popularity, and anything else that would get in the way of the life He would give. Dietrich Bonhoeffer has said, "When Jesus calls a man, he bids him come and die." [58] And yes, that can include even our physical life. This can be more than a little frightening to us, for many of us have much we think we have to hang on to. But there is such freedom in the eternal life Jesus gives.

Years ago, I worked with a woman who was dying of cancer. She and her husband were faithful believers who really loved each other. She had come to her last couple of months and was working through the difficult task of letting go.

Now this woman had always loved clothing and jewelry. It wasn't that she bought too many expensive things or was a bad steward of money. She just loved bright colors and found a great deal of joy in a bright, cheerful appearance. One day she said to me quite contentedly, "Pastor, I am ready to go. My dresses, that jewelry, it doesn't matter to me anymore. I'm ready to give it up. There's just one thing that I can't give up yet: my husband. I'm worried about how he will do after I'm gone."

Now that was a painful thing for her to say and for me to hear. There is nothing we hold dearer than our families. We love our spouses and our children. We take our children to school when they are young, and they take us to the doctor when we are old. We take pictures over the years and smile at the hairstyles for years to come. We go through all the joys and sorrows of life together. We hold each other when no one else will. And when death comes, we have to give those people up.

It broke my heart to hear her say that. And yet, she was right on the money. How could we come to grips with this? We prayed together, asking God to give us wisdom, comfort, and peace.

The next week when we talked together, our conversation centered around what it meant to really trust the Lord in this matter. She realized that her husband was not her own, that he was and always had been in the care of Jesus. If Jesus had watched over him all these years, He wasn't going to stop now.

Remember, Mary and Martha had some of these same feelings as they watched their brother die. But when Jesus raised him from the dead, He also gave them freedom. He helped them to realize that Lazarus' life was and had always been in the hands of their Savior. All of their lives were held in the hands of the God who would take on our sin and our death. His hands would be pierced with nails so that He could hold us safely, not just in this life, but for eternity.

Your life is also in those nail-scarred hands. You don't have to hang on to your possessions. You don't have to grasp for power or position. You don't even have to possess the people you love in your life. Jesus has you, and them, safe in His embrace.

And let me tell you, Jesus has big arms! These arms were big enough to carry our sins to the cross. His arms are big enough to carry any worry or fear you might have. And His arms are big enough to embrace many more people. His heart has room for many more of His lost children.

This is God's really big idea! He wants to bring all of humanity back to Himself. He wants to recover what was lost in the Garden of Eden when Adam and Eve sinned. He wants to replace our fears with faith, our conflicts with peace, our death with life. We were scattered from God and from each other when sin and death entered the world. God entered the world in Jesus to turn that around, to gather "*the scattered children of God, to bring them together and make them one.*" He would do that by giving His life.

The Great Rescuer

Hurricane Katrina hit the Southern coast of the United States August 29, 2005. It was the largest natural disaster ever experienced in the United States. When the storm hit, winds up to 145 miles per hour didn't just rip the roofs off of houses, they flattened entire dwellings. The roof of the New Orleans Superdome was partially torn off. A storm surge of water, over 20 feet high in some places, demolished houses, deposited floating businesses hundreds of yards inland, and ended the lives of many. It was a terrible disaster.

The days that followed were equally horrible. Lake Pontchartrain, to the north of New Orleans, broke through its levees and flooded the city. Fighting for their lives, people were stranded on rooftops. Some of them lost that fight. In the days that followed, water, food, and shelter were scarce. Looting and violence arose. The weakest of the weak—infants, the elderly, and the disabled—paid the highest price. Bodies were left floating in the water or on the sidewalks where they died. Even inside shelters, the aged and infants died side by side from dehydration and were simply placed against the walls. Human beings were scattered, lost, and dying.

This is an accurate picture of what sin and death do to us. It is not pretty. You cannot hide from it forever. Sin has scattered humanity around the globe. We cannot survive without the God who gives life, yet our sin separates us from Him. The stormy winds of our failures and the flood of our transgressions leave us condemned to a physical life where we all will die. These forces would condemn us to an eternal death of separation from God if we had no hope.

But God has sent a rescuer, an agent of life. John 11:52 says that Jesus died "*for the scattered children of God, to bring them together and make them one.*"

In New Orleans, in the midst of the dying, there were life-saving rescues happening before our eyes. Helicopters were lifting people from rooftops, saving them from the floodwaters. Many elderly were being carried by boats to safety. And in the two hospitals that were still functioning, the staffs stayed behind to care for the patients.

I saw one story about a neo-natal unit in a hospital that was very touching. Because these children were too fragile to evacuate, the medical and maintenance staff had stayed. During the storm, they moved these premature babies down a few floors, to protect them in case the wind damaged the upper floors. In the days that followed, everyone stayed to watch over and protect them, even in the face of dwindling resources and the danger of looters.

Jesus is the great Rescuer of humanity. He reaches out to those drowning in sin with His gracious forgiveness. To those living in the fear of death, He gives life. Through the power of His Word, He heals hearts, souls, minds and bodies. And at the time of death, He brings ultimate healing and ushers us into eternity. In His death and resurrection, we live.

> *"Since the children have flesh and blood, he too shared in their humanity so that by his death he might destroy him who holds the power of death—that is, the devil—and free those who all their lives were held in slavery by their fear of death."* [59]

Chapter 14

The Last Stone

At the beginning of this journey through John 11, we realized together that death is not just a statistic, especially when it touches someone we care about. When we face the death of a person we love, and particularly when we face our own death, it becomes a very personal struggle.

I want you to know that this is true for me, too. Death is not a detached, abstract concept in my life. As I finish writing this book, I have a sister who is dealing with very serious cancer. With the kind of cancer she has and the degree to which it has spread, she is facing a very serious opponent at the young age of 47. I struggle at times with feelings of sorrow and helplessness, feelings that I think all of us have when we face illness, dying, and death.

Every one of us is on an earthly journey that will end in death (unless Jesus returns before we die). Every one of us will take that difficult walk through the valley of the shadow of death.

But that walk is not the end of the story. Jesus does not deal with death in the abstract. To Him, death is not a concept; it is an experience. Jesus walked through that dark valley to bring light and life. On His back was a burden—the burden of our sin, the sin that brings death. It was a burden He carried alone to the bitter end on the cross. What joy we have in knowing a Savior who has brought real, eternal life for you and me! Earthly, physical death, as painful as it can be for all involved, is not the sad conclusion to a hopeless life for those who trust in Jesus.

On His cross sin was taken care of. Jesus cried out in triumph, "*It is finished.*" His work was finished. Sin was finished. In His resurrection, death met its match. These enemies, as powerful as they really are, no longer rule over you and me. At our baptisms, Jesus called us from the graves of our sin. We can live without wearing the grave clothes of a life devoid of hope, a life lived helplessly waiting for inevitable death. Death can no longer hold on to us, any more than death could hold on to Jesus. His resurrection is ours. His eternal life is ours.

Someday, Jesus will call your body out of the grave, even as He called Lazarus out of his. He will say to you "Come forth!" And you will. Every person who has ever lived will listen to the voice of the One who is the resurrection and the life. Jesus will open every graveyard, every cemetery, and every place where death has reached out its cold hand and robbed us of life. And the Lord of life will gather His people into life forever. The last enemy will have been permanently defeated, removed, and destroyed. The last stone in front of the last grave will be opened, and we will live!

> Jesus lives, the vict'ry's won,
> Death no longer can appall me.
> Jesus lives, death's reign is done,
> From the grave will he recall me.
> Brighter scenes will then commence.
> This shall be my confidence. [60]

Notes

1. Genesis 2:2
2. Genesis 2:16–17
3. Genesis 3:4–5
4. Genesis 3:6
5. Genesis 3:19
6. Romans 5:12
7. Romans 8:20–21
8. John 11:1
9. Romans 5:12
10. John 11:2–3
11. John 11:3–6
12. For these marvelous stories, see Mark 5:22–43 and Luke 7:11–17.
13. Matthew 26:39
14. John 11:7–8
15. John 11:11–13
16. John 11:48–50
17. Romans 8:38–39
18. 2 Corinthians 11:24–28
19. See Revelation 1:18
20. John 11:14–15
21. Hebrews 12:2
22. Luke 9:23
23. Romans 6:4
24. John 11:18–19
25. John 11:21–22

26. John 11:25–26
27. Genesis 1:1
28. Genesis 2:7
29. John 6:47
30. This story is found in Mark 5:22–34.
31. See Leviticus 15:25–27 and 2 Chronicles 23:18–19.
32. See, for example, John 9:1–3.
33. John 11:28
34. Romans 8:26
35. John 1:1, 14
36. Mark 15:32
37. 1 John 4:10
38. *Lutheran Service Book: Agenda*, prepared by the Commission on Worship of the Lutheran Church—Missouri Synod (Concordia Publishing House, 2006), p. 123
39. Psalm 116:15
40. John 11:38–39
41. Genesis 50:2, 26
42. Romans 6:23
43. Luke 18:19
44. John 11:39–41
45. Matthew 28:2
46. Romans 6:4–5
47. John 11:42
48. John 11:44
49. See John 19:38–40 and Mark 15:43–46.
50. 2 Peter 3:9
51. *The Every-day Life of Abraham Lincoln*, p. 578
52. Isaiah 7:14, Matthew 1:22–23
53. Micah 5:2, Matthew 2:5–6
54. John 11:45
55. John 11:47–48
56. John 11:49–53
57. Matthew 20:28
58. *The Cost of Discipleship*, Collier Books, p. 99
59. Hebrews 2:14–15

60. This verse is taken from a hymn written by Christian Gellert, translated into English by Frances E. Cox. It is based on John 14:19.

Questions for Thought and Discussion

Introduction *The Valley*

1. What do you treasure about God's gift of life? What experiences have you found most fulfilling?

2. What experiences are you still looking forward to? Marriage? Grandchildren? Retirement?

3. What are some of the questions and anxieties you have about facing death?

Chapter 1   *9-1-1*

1. Have you ever dialed 9-1-1? What were the circumstances? How did you feel?

2. Romans 5:12–21 tells us the cause of death—but also offers us hope in the Christ. Has death battered you and put you in need of hope? Read these verses and rejoice in God's gift of life.

3. Read Romans 8:26. What confidence can we have when we pray in the midst of a crisis?

Chapter 2   *Statistics Have Names*

1. Was there a time in your life when death went from being an impersonal matter to something very personal? How did you feel the first time someone you really loved died?

2. Take a look at Matthew 10:29–31. How do these verses remind you that you matter to God, that you are not a statistic to Him?

3. Read Hebrews 4:14–16. Why can we be confident when we pray?

Chapter 3   *Is God on Vacation?*

1. What circumstances make you feel most alone, distant even from God? Why is it sometimes hard to trust God when we feel pain or loss?

2. Take a look at Psalm 130. How does the Psalm writer express his longing for God? How is God's forgiveness our hope as we face death? You might memorize these words. Psalm 42 can also be a very helpful prayer during times of loss and sorrow.

3. Who is the main focus of your life? Who will be the main focus when you die? See Philippians 1:20–21 and Hebrews 12:2.

Chapter 4   *In Harm's Way*

1. In John 15:13, Jesus says, *"Greater love has no one than this, that he lay down his life for his friends."* How does it feel to know that Jesus laid down His life for you—that He considers you His friend?

2. Do you know someone who needs to hear the news that Jesus can wake someone even from death? Pray for an opportunity to share with them God's gift of eternal life.

3. Consider memorizing Romans 8:38–39. What kind of certainty and confidence for living and dying does Jesus give to us?

Chapter 5   *The News Nobody Wants*

1. What feelings do you have when you consider your own death? What hope does Isaiah 26:19 give you?

2. Have you known a Christian who gave a powerful witness at the time of death? How might the preamble to your will or living trust allow you to give such a witness?

3. How have so many Christians up to this day been able to die for their faith? See Mark 13:11–13.

Chapter 6   *Just Show Up*

1. The last time you attended a funeral or memorial service to support a friend or family member, did you struggle to find words to say? How did you feel?

2. Read 2 Corinthians 1:3–5. How can it be helpful to quietly share the grief of a friend?

3. See 1 Corinthians 12:26–27 and Romans 12:15. What person has God used to come to you "with skin on"?

Chapter 7   *Where Is the Resurrection?*

1. What are some of the things you are tempted to turn to when you are in pain? Take some time to read and meditate on Psalm 42.

2. When is it hard for you to trust Jesus?

3. Have you ever thought of the resurrection as a Person, as Jesus? What joy does this bring? See John 6:47.

Chapter 8   *If Only You Had Been Here*

1. Have you ever avoided Jesus during a time of pain? What led you to do this?

2. Read Luke 15. How does God feel about lost people? What does He do? See also Luke 19:10.

3. How does it help to know that Jesus understands pain?

Chapter 9   *A Companion on the Road of Grief*

1. Have you ever felt so sad and so lonely that you didn't think anyone, even God, could understand? Read Psalm 25 and Romans 8:26 to hear about the comfort God gives.

2. Read Psalm 116. What reasons to praise God do you find here?

3. What does it mean to you that Jesus cried at the grave of Lazarus?

Chapter 10   *Take Away the Stone*

1. Can you remember the first time someone you really cared about died? What emotions went through you?

2. Have you ever gone to a viewing at a funeral home? How did you feel when you saw the body of the person who had died?

3. Read Romans 6:5. How can you thank God today for the eternal life He gives you?

Chapter 11   *Thankful in the Midst of Death?*

1. Read Hebrews 12:2. How does it make you feel to know that saving you was a cause of great joy for Jesus?

2. What Bible verses would you want to be read at your memorial service? Take some time to talk with your pastor about a service for you when you die.

3. How can we be thankful, even as we face death? See 1 Corinthians 15:19–20.

Chapter 12   *Lazarus, Come Out!*

1. Have you ever been involved in a traffic accident? What sort of emotions did you feel? What sort of emotions do you feel when you see death approaching a loved one?

2. Read John 11:43–44. What comfort can we find in the strong, commanding tone Jesus uses here?

3. Consider memorizing John 6:40, and share it with someone who needs the hope that Jesus brings.

Chapter 13   *A Matter of Life and Death*

1. Jesus makes some very bold claims about His identity in John 11 and elsewhere (see John 8:58, for example). Who do you believe Jesus is? How does that show in your life?

2. In Mark 8:35, Jesus calls us to let go of the control of our lives. What area of your life do you find most difficult to give up to Jesus? Where has Jesus given you strength to let go?

3. Who do you know that needs to be rescued by Jesus? Start praying for that person today, and ask God to give you a chance to share the love of Jesus with him or her.

Chapter 14   *The Last Stone*

1. What comfort do you find in knowing that death is not the end for all who trust in Jesus?

2. What person in your life needs to have this hope? How can you share with this person the hope Jesus gives?

3. Consider carrying a small stone in your pocket or purse for the next few weeks. Use it to remind you of the victory Jesus has won over death.

Appendix

Helping a friend through death. What can I do?

Facing your own death or the death of a friend or family member can be very difficult. The feelings of anger, fear, separation, depression and loneliness can be very intense, even frightening. Romans 12:15 tells us *"to mourn with those who mourn."* How can we do this?

Pray.   When we talk to God in prayer, He answers. Put the name of your friend on your daily prayer list. Ask your friend what you can specifically pray about, and pray each day.

Listen.   A person suffering through grief needs to pour out the pain, and we need to listen. Answers are not always required.

Provide.   Be ready to provide resources when your friend needs them. The Bible passages and books listed here can be a place to begin. A local congregation with an active Stephen Ministry can provide a compassionate listener to come alongside. Your pastor can be a very helpful resource, and should be able to recommend a good Christian counselor, if the need arises.

Remember, Jesus walks us through the valley of the shadow of death. He is with your friend, and He will walk with the two of you as you journey together through the pain.

Jesus said to her, "I am the resurrection and the life. He who believes in me will live, even though he dies; and whoever lives and believes in me will never die."

Scripture References

For millennia, God has strengthened His people through His living and active Word. There are many additional Bible passages beyond the ones I have listed here, but these will get you started. I encourage you to read the references, meditate on them in prayer, and commit to memory the verses that are especially meaningful to you.

Job 19:25-27	Psalm 4	Psalm 22
Psalm 23	Psalm 42	Psalm 96
Psalm 98	Psalm 130	Psalm 145
Isaiah 25:6-9	Matthew 28:1-10	Luke 24
John 20	John 5:21-29	Romans 8:31-39
1 Corinthians 15	Philippians 3:20-21	Revelation 1:17-18
Revelation 7:9-17	Revelation 21:1-5	Revelation 22:1-7

Books to read

Billy Graham, *Facing Death and the Life After* (Minneapolis, MN: Grason, 1987)
This book answers a lot of questions about death from a Biblical perspective.
www.amazon.com

Craig Parrott, *For the Faint of Heart: Hope For The Hurting* (Xulon Press, 2003)
This is an excellent book to give to a friend who has questions about death or suffering in general, written in a conversational style.
www.cph.org

Joanne Marxhausen, *Heaven Is A Wonderful Place* (St. Louis, Concordia Publishing House, 2004)
Written to encourage young children who are facing the death of loved ones, this book presents the hope of eternal life from the Bible.
www.cph.org

What others have said about *Take Away the Stone:*

"This book was written from a pastor's heart and personal experience with death and dying as an encouragement to others…. The reader will find redemption and comfort for one of life's toughest challenges—facing death with hope."

> - Marlene Woertz, Licensed Marriage and Family Therapist

"If your journey through life has been brutally interrupted by the death of someone close to you or by the inevitability of your own passing, you must read this book. Outside the Bible, I know of no book that better shows how God has swallowed up death and given us the victory through our Lord Jesus Christ."

> - Craig Parrott, Spiritual Director, Denver Lutheran High School, and author of *For the Faint of Heart*

"Despite our advances in science, health, and medicine, death, our ancient enemy, still stalks our lives, seeking to destroy all that we count good and hold dear. It's in the midst of death's shadow that Alan Sommer offers a wonderful, pastoral gift. Tracing the footsteps of Jesus in John 11, he takes us on a faith building journey that leads us through the dark valley to the very heart of God and the eternal life He offers to all. Having walked with Alan through its pages, I commend this book as a faithful guide in group Bible study or personal devotion, knowing that it will bring the reader to the irrevocable conclusion that God, not death, speaks the last and lasting word on our lives."

> - Dr. Robert Newton, District President, California-Nevada-Hawaii District, Lutheran Church – Missouri Synod

"Caregivers face the pain death brings and sometimes struggle to bring God's comfort and answers to grieving people. *Take Away the Stone* offers the opportunity for both caregiver and care receiver to make the journey from devastation and defeat to peace, joy and confidence."

> - Alison Dumas, Stephen Minister and Stephen Ministry Leader

"You will walk away from *Take Away the Stone* with the understanding that all of us can experience eternal life through Christ the Lord and not have to fear death again."

> - Jan Marie Peeples, recently widowed

"This book gives strength to those who are facing death because it proclaims the One who is our strength, Jesus the Christ."

> - Aaron Smith, Pastor of St. Paul Lutheran Church, Mtn. View, CA

Printed in the United States
201929BV00003B/229-1323/P